PHARMACEUTICAL JURISPRUDENCE

SECOND YEAR DIPLOMA IN PHARMACY

According to the PCI New Education Regulations, 1991

PHARMACEUTICAL JURISPRUDENCE

SECOND YEAR DIPLOMA IN PHARMACY

According to the PCI New Education Regulations, 1991

Neerja Gandhi
M.Pharm.
College of Pharmacy
Pushp Vihar, Delhi University

Harvinder Popli
M.Pharm. Ph.D., F.I.C.A.
College of Pharmacy
Pushp Vihar, Delhi University

CBSPD

CBS Publishers & Distributors Pvt Ltd

New Delhi • Bengaluru • Chennai • Kochi • Kolkata • Lucknow • Mumbai
Hyder8abad • Jharkhand • Nagpur • Patna • Pune • Uttarakhand

Disclaimer

Science and technology are constantly changing fields. New research and experience broaden the scope of information and knowledge. The authors have tried their best in giving information available to them while preparing the material for this book. Although, all efforts have been made to ensure optimum accuracy of the material, yet it is quite possible some errors might have been left uncorrected. The publisher, the printer and the authors will not be held responsible for any inadvertent errors or inaccuracies.

PHARMACEUTICAL JURISPRUDENCE

ISBN: 978-81-239-0552-5

First Edition : 1997

Reprint: 2001, 2002, 2004, 2005, 2006, 2008, 2009, 2010, 2012, 2015, 2017, 2018, 2019, 2023, **2025**

Published by Satish Kumar Jain and produced by Varun Jain for

CBS Publishers & Distributors Pvt Ltd

4819/XI Prahlad Street, 24 Ansari Road, Daryaganj, New Delhi 110 002, India

Ph: 011-23289259, 23266861 Website: www.cbspd.com e-mail: delhi@cbspd.com

Corporate Office: 204 FIE, Industrial Area, Patparganj, Delhi 110 092, India

Ph: 011-4934 4934 Fax: 011-4934 4935 e-mail: publishing@cbspd.com; publicity@cbspd.com

Branches

- **Bengaluru:** Seema House 2975, 17th Cross, KR Road, Banasankari 2nd Stage, Bengaluru 560 070, Karnataka, India
  Ph: +91-80-26771678/79 Fax: +91-80-26771680 e-mail: bangalore@cbspd.com
- **Chennai:** 7, Subbaraya Street, Shenoy Nagar, Chennai 600 030, Tamil Nadu, India
  Ph: +91-44-26680620, 26681266 Fax: +91-44-42032115 e-mail: chennai@cbspd.com
- **Kochi:** 42/1325, 1326, Power House Road, Opp KSEB, Power House, Ernakulam, Kochi 682 018, India
  Ph: +91-484-4059061-65 Fax: +91-484-4059065 e-mail: kochi@cbspd.com
- **Kolkata:** 147, Hind Ceramics Compound, 1st Floor, Nilgunj Road, Belghoria, Kolkata 700 056, West Bengal, India
  Ph: +91-33-25633055-56 e-mail: kolkata@cbspd.com
- **Lucknow:** Basement, Khushnuma Complex, 7-Meerabai Marg (behind Jawahar Bhawan), Lucknow 226 001, India
  Ph: +91-522-4000032 e-mail: tiwari.lucknow@cbspd.com
- **Mumbai:** PWD Shed. Gala no. 25/26, Ramchandra Bhatt Marg, Next to JJ Hospital Gate no. 2, Opp. Union Bank of India, Noorbaug Mumbai 400 009, Maharashtra, India
  Ph: +91-22-66661880/89 e-mail: mumbai@cbspd.com

Representatives

• **Hyderabad**	0-9885175004	• **Jharkhand**	0-9811541605	• **Nagpur**	0-9421945513
• **Patna**	0-9334159340	• **Pune**	0-9923910676	• **Uttarakhand**	0-9716462459

Printed at Sanjay Printers, Sahibabad, UP, India

Preface

In the present era of globalisation, the job of a pharmacist is becoming challenging day by day. As per the new Education Regulation (ER 91), the importance of Forensic Pharmacy has increased. This book fulfills the main purpose from the point of view of students and teachers as various aspects of Forensic Pharmacy covering laws related to drugs have been covered in simple language. We have tried our best to make this book compact.

We are highly thankful to Mr. S.K. Jain and his team (CBS Publishers & Distributors) for his cooperation in bringing the book out in such a short span of time.

We welcome any suggestions or comments for the improvement of this book.

Acknowledgement : We are greatly thankful to Mr. D.D. Bakshi, ex-staffer of The Hindustan Times for assisting in simplification and compilation of text material.

—*Authors*

Syllabus for D.Pharma. II Year
Pharmaceutical Jurisprodence

Theory (50 hours)

1. Origin and nature of Pharmaceutical legislation in India, its scope and objectives. Evolution of the "Concept of Pharmacy" as an integral part of the Health Care System.
2. Principles and significance of professional ethics. Critical study of the code of pharmaceutical ethics drafted by Pharmacy Council of India.
3. Pharmacy Act, 1948—The General study of the Pharmacy Act with special reference to Education Regulations, working of State and General Central Councils, constitution of these councils and functions. Registration procedures under the Act.
4. The Drugs and Cosmetics Act, 1940—General study of the Drugs and Cosmetics Act and the Rules thereunder. Definitions and salient features related to retail and wholesale distribution of drugs. The powers of Inspectors, the sampling procedures and the procedure and formalities in obtaining licences under the rule. Facilities to be provided for running a pharmacy effectively. General study of the schedule with special reference of schedules C, C_1, F, G, J, H, P and X and salient features of labelling and storage condition of drugs.
5. The Drugs and Magic Remedies (Objectionable Advertisement) Act, 1954—General study of the Act. Objectives, special reference to be laid on Advertisements. Magic remedies and objectionable and permitted advertisements—disease which cannot be claimed to be cured.
6. Narcotic Drugs and Psychotropic Substances Act, 1985—A brief study of the Act with special reference to its objectives, offences and punishment.

7. Brief introduction to the study of the following acts:
   (1) Latest Drugs (Price Control) Order in force.
   (2) Poisons Act, 1919 (as amended to date).
   (3) Medicinal and Toilet Preparations (Excise Duties) Act, 1955 (as amended to date).
   (4) Medical Termination of Pregnancy Act, 1971 (as amended to date).

Syllabus for B.Pharma. I Year (Delhi Univ.)

Forensic Pharmacy and Ethics

Theory (50 hours)

An objective study of the following :

(a) Drugs and Cosmetics Act, 1940 and rules made thereunder

(b) The Dangerous Drugs Act, 1930

(c) The Pharmacy Act, 1948

(d) The Drugs and Magic Remedies (Objectionable Advertisement) Act, 1954

(e) Medicinal and Toilet Preparations (Excise Duties) Act, 1955

(f) The Drugs (Price Control) Order, 1979

(g) The Shops Act of the State

(h) The Medical Termination of Pregnancy Act, 1971

(i) The Poisons Act, 1919

(j) The Prevention of Cruelty to Animals Act

(k) The Insecticides Act

(l) The Code of Pharmaceutical Ethics framed by Pharmacy Council of India

Contents

1

CONCEPT OF LAW AND PHARMACEUTICAL LEGISLATION IN INDIA

INTRODUCTION

In the ancient times there were no written laws to control pharmacy and medicines legally. Scientific techniques were not used either in the manufacture or standardisation of medicines. Impirical techniques were more prevalent. Ancient system of medicine was the oldest to be practised in India. Unani and Tibbi system gained patronization during Muslim rulers. After the entry of British traders in India Western or allopathic system gained patronage and during that time most of the drugs were imported.

Development during 19th and 20th centuries various laws and rules have been framed. Following points need to be highlighted.

— Spurious and substandard drugs became more common.

— Adulterated drugs and quack medicines manufactured in different parts of world were being dumped in India to be sold by unqualified persons.

— Poisoning due to overdosage, inaccurate usage of adulterated and spurious drugs resulted in poisoning.

— There was no machinery to control over malpractises undergoing as amplified by Indian Medical Gazette during 1927-29, Drugs Enquiry Committee Report 1931, Indian Medical Gazette Sept. 1927 and July 1929.

— Various reports revealed that there was no rigid control over the nature and quality of drugs; import or manufacture of sub-standard drugs. India was truly the land of quacks.

— For all practical purposes, except Poision Act 1919, there were no laws to regulate import, manufacture or sell the therapeutic substances to public.

— Certain laws for e.g. Indian Merchandise Marks Act 1889 had indirect control over the drugs regarding misbranding of goods, false mark upon the containers of goods, deceiving any person in regard to type, nature or quality of drugs. Apart from this Sea Customs Act 1898 and Indian Tariff Act of 1894 provided for levying of customs duty on goods which included chemicals and medicines also imported into Indian or exported from the country. The Opium Act 1878 dealt with the cultivation of poppy including manufacture, possession transport, import, export and sale. Poison Act 1919 only dealt with the regulation of import, possession and sale of poisons. Another Act namely Cantonment Act of 1929 empowered the authorities to enter into any shop and seize any medicine considered adulterated.

— In addition to the above mentioned Acts, in different states of India enactment of different Acts controlled adulteration of drugs. For Punjab Pure Food Act 1929, the Punjab Municipal Act 1911, The Punjab Excise Act 1914, Bihar and Orissa Municipal Act 1922, Bombay City Municipal Act 1888 and 1925, Bengal Municipal Act 1884, Bengal Food Adulteration Act 1919, Bengal Excise Act 1909 etc.

— On comparing the affairs regarding pharmacy in India and other developed countries, it is quite evident that countries like United Kingdom, The United States of America, Canada etc. are much above us regarding the fair trade practice in pharmaceuticals for e.g. Therapeutic Substances Act of 1925 and Food and Drugs (Adulteration) Act of 1928 in the United Kingdom fully safeguarded the interests of people of Britain. While in United States of America, the Federal Food and Drugs Act, 1906 amended and reamended in 1912, 1915 and 1927 effectively prohibited the manufacture, sale, transshipment of adultrated, misbranded, poisonous or deleterious drugs and medicines. Food and Drugs Act of 1920 and the Patent and Proprietary Medicines (amended in 1919) in Canada regulated and controlled Drugs and Medicinal preparations.

DRUGS ENQUIRY COMMITTEE

Government of India on 11th August 1930, appointed a committee under the chairmanship of Late Col. R.N. Chopra to see into the problems of pharmacy. The main aims of the committee were :

(1) To enquire into the extent to which drugs and chemicals of impure quality and defective strength particularly those recognised by British Pharmacopoeia. are imported, manufactured or sold in British India and the necessity in the public interest of controlling such importation, manufacture and sale to make recommendations.

(2) To report how far the recommendations made in (1) may be extended to known and approved medical preparations other than those referred to above, and to medicines made from indigenous drugs and chemicals.

(3) To enquire into the necessity of legislation to restrict the profession of pharmacy to duly qualified persons and to make recommendations.

The report of this historic committee was published in

1931 after thorough investigations and extensive tour of the country. Some experts from the committee's report reveal the following :

- There is no organised or self-contained profession of pharmacy in India in the sense in which it exists in other parts of the world.
- Profession is represented by a set of people known as compounders whose status, functions and duties are ill defined and improperly understood.
- They handle the drugs and poisons with utmost ease and freedom ignoring their properties and potency.
- They carry on compounding, dispensing and selling of drugs and chemicals from day to day.
- They do work of dressers, laboratory assistants anaethetist and operation assistants also and list of such manifold duties also include posing as a physician sometimes.
- They have low standard of education and professional training cannot impart the skills expected.
- No stress is laid as to the basic qualifications except in recently revised Compounder's Course in Bengal and Chemist Druggist Course in Madras.

This Drug Enquiry Committee is an important document as it initiated an era of pharmaceutical uprising in the country but it failed to influence the Government for immediate action. Just after its publication Prof. Mahadeva Lal Shroff initiated education of pharmacy in B.H.U. Following this many universities introduced Bachelor's degree of Pharmacy. In 1937, first Indian Pharmaceutical Association known as the United Provinces Pharmaceutical Association was organised at Banaras. In due course of time the neglected profession of pharmacy started gaining footing. A journal Indian and Eastern Chemist started getting published from India (Calcutta) as well as London. The demand for the betterment of pharmaceutical conditions in India was being supported even in the Pharmaceutical Journal and the Chemist and Druggist of England.

Further improvements in this regard are listed as follows:

— In 1936, the Indian Journal of Pharmacy started by Prof. Shroff under the auspices of U.P. Pharmaceutical Association which was later known as Indian Pharmaceutical Association.

— In 1940, the Indian Pharmaceutical Association initiated All India Pharmaceutical Conference and it held sessions in different states of the country to awaken the people all over India.

— Various problems of pharmacy were taken up by public at all levels.

— Various Acts which came into force after the publication of Drugs Enquiry Committee Report are following :

— In 1937, Government of India brought forth the "Import of Drugs Bill" after 7 years of the Report. This was strongly criticised by The Indian and Eastern Chemist Feb. 1938, so Government had to withdraw the Bill ultimately due to high criticism.

— In 1940, the Drugs Bill was brought in force to regulate the import, manufacture, sale and distribution of drugs in India. It was submitted to a selected committee and after modification it was finally adopted as Drugs Act 1940. For the purpose of Act—

  a) The first Drugs Technical Advisory Board (DTAB) was formed in 1941.

  b) Central Drugs Laboratory was reconstituted instead of the Biochemical Standardization Laboratory of Calcutta.

— Drugs rules were framed in 1945 and published under Drugs Act 1940. The provisions of Act now cover Cosmetics, Ayurvedic, Unani and Homocopathic medicines.

— In 1945, the Pharmacy Bill was brought forth by the Government. It became Pharmacy Act 1948 after full three years.

— In 1949, the first Pharmacy Council of India was constituted under the Act. The Act provided that within three years of its passage, the Pharmacy Councils in each state should be constituted and Education Regulation should take effect within next three years.

— In 1954, the Drugs and Magic Remedies (Objectionable Advertisement) Act was passed and enforced to counteract unsocial and misleading advertisements.

— Different set of excise duty, in different states resulted in great handicap in the progress of Indian drug industry involving spirituous medicinal preparations. So considering this, a uniform law was enforced for the whole country in 1955. This was Medicinal and Toilet Preparations (Excise Duties) Act.

— In 1985 a comprehensive Act namely Narcotic and Psychotropic Substances Act has been enacted to protect society from dangers of addictive drugs followed by another complementary Act namely Prevention of Illicit Traffic in Psychotropic Substance Act 1988.

— Drugs Enquiry Committee had recommended the compilation of the Indian Pharmacopoeia with monographs on drugs and pharmaceuticals. Under the Chairmanship of Late Col. R.N. Chopra, a committee was appointed in 1944 and in 1946, the Indian pharmacopoeial list was published under the auspices of this committee. Aftermath a full fledged Indian pharmacopoeia committee was constituted in 1948 under the chairmanship of Late Dr. B.N. Ghosh of Calcutta alongwith several sub committees.

— In 1955 first edition of the Indian Pharmacopoeia was published. In 1966 corrected and enhanced second edition of Indian pharmacopoeia was published.

2

CODE OF PHARMACEUTICAL ETHICS AS DRAFTED BY PHARMACY COUNCIL OF INDIA

INTRODUCTION

Code of Pharmaceutical Ethics as formulated by Pharmacy Council of India which are meant to guide the pharmacist as to how he should conduct himself, in relation to himself, his patrons, general public, co-professional etc.

Ethics means the 'code of moral principles' or it may be defined as the science/philosophy of moral values or moral norms.

It is mainly emphasised on the determination of right or wrong, while doing one's duty.

In short, it is mainly concerned with the right way of conducting in daily life which should be governed by moral rules of human behaviour.

Profession of pharmacy is a noble profession as it is indirectly healing the persons to get well with the help of medical practitioners and other co-professionals. So it has the responsibility of safeguarding the people's health.

Government has already restricted the practice of pharmacy to only professionals i.e. registered pharmacist under the Pharmacy Act 1948. But in this age of modernisation there is a definite need of formulating ethical code for every profession of life including pharmacy. So Pharmacy Council of India has formulated the code of pharmaceutical ethics to set general guidelines for the Indian pharmacists.

A Pharmacist above all must be a good citizen to defend the laws of the state and the country. He has to uphold above all the interest of his patrons and people.

According to pharmaceutical ethics the following points are to be noted for the pharmacist as framed by PCI.

1. Pharmacist in relation to his job.
2. Pharmacist in relation to his trade.
3. Pharmacist in relation to medical profession.
4. Pharmacist in relation to his profession.

1. PHARMACIST IN RELATION TO HIS JOB

Following are things which a pharmacist should keep in mind while dealing in relation to his job.

(i) PHARMACEUTICAL SERVICES

It is essential that reasonably comprehensive pharmaceutical services should be provided when the premises are registered under statutory requirements and are opened as a pharmacy. This involves supply of emergency medicines at all times according to the need of the public in addition to supplying commonly required medicines without undue delay;

(ii) CONDUCT OF THE PHARMACY

Error of accidental contamination in the preparation, dispensing and supply of medicines should be checked in a pharmacy.

(a) The professional character of the pharmacy should be represented by the appearance of the premises clearly indicating to the public that the practice of pharmacy is being carried out in the establishment.

(b) At the premises a notice indicating and stating that

dispensing is carried out under Employees State Insurance Scheme (E.S.I.S.) or any other similar scheme sponsored by the Government should be exhibited.

(c) Every pharmacy should be personally controlled by a pharmacist.

(d) An owner of a pharmacy will be regarded as a failure in observance of the standards of conduct, if he put any obstruction to the execution of the duties of a pharmacist.

(iii) HANDLING OF PRESCRIPTION

(a) A pharmacist should receive a prescription presented to him for dispensing it without any discussion or comment over it as regards the merits and demerits of its therapeutic efficiacy.

(b) He should neither show any physiognomic expression of alarm on receipt of a prescription because these things are liable to cause anxiety in patients or their agents and shake their faith in the capabilities of the physician.

(c) Careful handling is needed in answering any Question on a prescription.

(d) The pharmacist should neither add, omit or substitute any ingredient nor alter the composition of a prescription without the consent of the prescriber until and unless the change is emergent and is required purely by the pharmaceutical technique without causing any alteration in the therapeutic action of the recipe or prescription.

(e) The prescription should always be referred back to the prescriber for correction and approval of the change suggested if any due to any error ommission or compatibility or over dose.

(f) The patient should be advised by the pharmacist to use medicines or remedies strictly in accordance with intention of the physician.

(iv) HANDLING OF DRUGS

(a) A prescription should always be dispensed correctly and carefully by weighing and measuring all ingredients in correct proposition by means of scales and measures.

(b) Visual estimations should be avoided.

(c) Substandard and unethical preparations should never be used to fill the prescription.

(d) Only drugs and medicinal preparations of standard quality should always be used.

(e) If there is any reason to believe that such drugs are required for any abusive purpose of addition, these should not be supplied to any one.

(v) APPRENTICE PHARMACIST

A pharmacist who is incharge of a dispensary, drug store or hospital, pharmacy where apprentice pharmacists are admitted for practical training should see that they are provided full facilities for their work for making them dependable pharmacists on completion of their training by acquiring sufficient techniques and skills of pharmacy. Moreover, until and unless the trainee has proved himself worthy of the certificate or credentials and above criterion for training is adopted no certificate or credentials should be granted to him.

2. PHARMACIST IN RELATION TO HIS TRADE

Following are the provisions which pharmacist should keep in mind while dealing with his trade :

(i) PRICE STRUCTURE

The prices charged should be fair and in keeping with the quality and quantity of commodity supplied as well as labour and skill required in making it ready for use.

(ii) FAIR TRADE PRACTICE

(a) Fair practice should be adopted by a pharmacist in the trade without any attempt to capture the business of a contemporary by cut throat competitions.

(b) If a customer brings by mistake an order or prescription to a dispensary genuinly intended to be served by some other dispensary, the pharmacist should refuse to accept it and should direct the customer to the right place.

(c) Imitation or copying of the labels, trade marks and other signs as well as symbols of the contemporaries should not be done.

(iii) PURCHASE OF DRUGS

(a) the pharmacist should always be careful not to aid or abet directly or indirectly the manufacture, possession, distribution and sale of spurious or substandard drugs. He should always purchase the drugs from genuine and reputable sources.

(b) Hawking of drugs and medicines should not be encouraged. The distribution of therapeutic substances without an expert supervision and highly undesireable technique of self medication, self service method of operating pharmacies should not be encouraged.

(iv) ADVERTISING AND DISPLAYS

The sale of medicines or medical appliances, display of materials in undignified style should not be used whether on the premises, in the press or elsewhere. Further, the medicines or medical appliances for sale to the public should not contain the following:

(a) Any wording, design or illustration which reflect unfavourably on pharmacists collectively as a group or on any individual.

(b) A disgracing references directly or by implication to other supplies, products, remedies or treatments.

(c) Misleading or exaggerated statements or claim.

(d) The word "Cure" in reference to an ailment or symptoms of ill health.

(e) A guarantee of therapeutic efficacy.

(f) An appeal of fear.

(g) An offer to refund the money paid.

(h) A price, competition or similar sale scheme.

(i) Any reference of a medical practitioner or a hospital or use of the words "Doctor" or "Dr. Nurse" alongwith the name of a new preparation not established previously.

(j) A reference to sexual weakness, premature ageing or loss of virility.

(k) A reference of complaints of sexual nature in terms lacking the proper reticence to the subject.

The following points should be noted :

(l) In a pharmacy, no article or preparation advertised to the public by means of display material of a type mentioned above should be exhibited after its advertisement.

(m) Contraceptive preparation and appliance or their illustration should not be exhibited. Only a notice approved by regulations and bearing the words "Family Planning Requisites" should be exhibited.

(n) Selling or distribution of lustful, obscene and indecent publications of any kind or description being highly harmful to the moral welfare of the nation should not be carried out under any circumstances.

3. PHARMACIST IN RELATION TO MEDICAL PROFESSION

Following are code of ethics of a pharmacist in relation to medical profession :

(i) LIMITATION OF PROFESSIONAL ACTIVITY

(a) The professional activity of the medical practitioner as well as the pharmacists should be limited to their own field.

(b) To avoid coded prescriptions and monopolistic practice detrimental to the pharmaceutical profession, the medical practitioners should not take to practice of pharmacy by owning drug stores.

(c) The pharmacist also should not take to medical practice of diagnosing diseases and prescribing remedies under any circumstances.

(d) A pharmacist can however render first aid to the victim in case of accidents and emergencies.

(ii) CLANDESTINE ARRANGEMENTS

A pharmacist should not enter into a clandestine or secret arrangements or contract with a physician by offering him any commission or any advantages.

(iii) LIAISON WITH PUBLIC

A pharmacist should always maintain proper liaison between medical profession and the people. He should advise the physicians on pharmaceutical matters like those of colours, vehicles and newer forms of administration of medicines and educate the people for maintaining healthy and sanitary conditions of living. For this purpose he should keep himself abreast with the modern developments in pharmacy and other allied sciences by regularly reading books, journals, magazines and other periodicals. Thus a pharmacist should at all times endeavour to promote knowledge and contribute his quota in the advancement of learning as well as contribute his share in nation building activity of the country.

Any information acquired by a pharmacist during his professional activities should not be disclosed to any third party or person until and unless required to do so by law. Further, any confidence reposed in a pharmacist by his patrons or won by him by virtue of his eminent character and conduct should not be lost by betraying them.

4. PHARMACIST IN RELATION TO HIS PROFESSION

As regards his profession, following code of ethics should be fulfilled:

(i) PROFESSIONAL VIGILANCE

A pharmacist in addition to himself being a law abiding and detering from doing things derogatory to the society and his profession, he should treat it his bounded duty to make others also to fulfill the provisions of the pharmaceutical and other laws and regulations. He should be fearless in bringing or causing a miscreant to be brought to book even if he is member of his own profession. He should be vigilant to weed the undesirable out of the profession and help to maintain its fair name and traditions even while extending help and co-operation to a fellow member in his legitimate needs, scientific, technical or otherwise.

(ii) Law-abiding Citizens

A pharmacist, who is engaged in profession of pharmacy

has to be an enlightened citizen with a fair knowledge of the laws of the land and he should be especially conversant with the enactments pretaining to food, drug, pharmacy, health, sanitation and the like and should abide by them in every phase of life. A pharmacist is a unit whole and his life cannot be divided into compartments.

(iii) Relationship with Professional Organisations

A Pharmacist should be actively involved in professional organisation in order to inculcate a corporate life in his own professional colleagues. A pharmacist should join and advance the cause of all such organisations, the aims and objects of which are conducive to scientific, moral well-being of pharmacists and at the same time in no way contrary to the code of pharmaceutical ethics.

(iv) Decorum and Propriety

A pharmacist should always restrict from doing all such acts and deeds which are not in consonance with the decorum and propriety of pharmaceutical profession and are likely to being discredit or upbraid to the profession or to himself.

(v) Pharmacists Oath

A young prospective pharmacist should feel no hesitation in assuming the following pharmacists Oath :

"I promise to do all I can to protect and improve the physical and moral well-being of society, holding the health and safety of my community above other considerations. I shall uphold the laws and standards governing my profession, avoiding all forms of misrepresentation, and I shall safeguard the distribution of medical and potent substances.

Knowledge gained about patients, I shall hold in confidence and never divulge unless compelled to do so by law.

I shall strive to perfect and enlarge my knowledge to contribute to the advancement of pharmacy and the public health.

I furthermore promise to maintain my honour in all transactions and by my conduct never bring discredit to myself or to my profession nor to do anything to diminish the trust reposed in my professional bretheren.

May I prosper and live long in favour as I keep and hold to this, my Oath, but if violate these sacred promises, may the reverse be my lot."

3

PHARMACY ACT

INTRODUCTION AND OBJECTIVE OF ACT

Pharmacy Act was passed in 1948 in order to raise the status of the profession of Pharmacy in India. For a long time the procurement, preparation and dispensing of drugs needed professional handling like medicine and nursing. But till the fifth decade of 20th century drug related operations were not under the strict control of any law. This included everything like handling, preparing, dispensing etc. Drugs Act which was passed in 1940 was the first step to upgrade and uplift the profession of pharmacy. Then after independence Pharmacy Act was passed in 1948. Compounder which included in the lowest category of health care team and people had the misleading concept in mind that anybody could read and give the medicine written on the prescription. It was not considered as a technical profession with the enforcement of Pharmacy Act which intends to whole of India except the State of Jammu and Kashmir, the pharmacy profession gained a status of its own.

DEFINITIONS

PHARMACY ACT 1948

(a) **Agreement :** means an agreement entered into under section 20.

(b) **Approved :** means approved by the central council under section 12 or section 14.

(c) **Central Council :** means the Pharmacy Council of India constituted under section 3.

(d) **Central Register :** means the register of pharmacists maintained by the central council under sec. 15A.

(i) **Executive Committee :** means the executive committee of the central council or of the state council as the context may require.

(e) **Indian Universtiy :** means a university within the meaning of sec. 3 of the University Grants Commission Act 1956 and includes such other institutions, being institutions established by or under a Central Act, as the Central Govt. notification in the official Gazette specified in this behalf.

(f) **Medical Practitioner :** means a person

(i) holding a qualification granted by an authority specified or notified under sec. 3 of the Indian Medical Degree Act 1916 or specified in the schedules to the Indian Medical Council Act 1956 or

(ii) Registered or eligible for registration in a medical register of a statement for the Registration of Persons practising the modern scientific system of medicine

(iii) registered in a medical register of a state who althrough not falling within sub clause (i) or sub-clause (ii) is declared by a general or special order made by the State Govt. in this behalf as a person practising the modern scientific system of medicine for the purpose of this Act.

(iv) registered or eligible for registration in the register of dentists for a state under the Dentists Act 1948

(v) who was engaged in the practise of veterinary medicine and who possesses qualifications approved by the state Govt.

(g) **Prescribed :** means in chapter (ii) prescribed by regulations made under section 18 and elsewhere prescribed by rules made under section 46.

(h) **Register :** means a register of pharmacists prepared and maintained under Chapter IV.

(i) **Registered Pharmacist :** means a person whose name is for the time being entered in the register of the state in which he is for the time being residing or carrying on his profession or business of pharmacy.

(j) **State Council :** means a state coucil of pharmacy constituted under sec. 19 and includes a point state council of pharmacy constituted in accordance with an agreement under sec. 20.

The Act was amended in 1959 and 1976. The image of pharmacy has totally changed in the present society. Pharmacists are equally respected as the other members of health care team.

Two main objectives of Pharmacy Act are,

(1) It frames the uniform education and training for the 'would be' pharmacist, to ensure that such persons have sufficient knowledge and technical skill for practising the profession as per the need of modern world.

(2) It also maintains the control the persons entering in the profession of pharmacy and restricts the practice of profession only by trained and qualified professionals.

Pharmacy Council of India : Constitution & Functions :

The Act has the provision for the constitution of a Central Council of Pharmacy called the Pharmacy Council of India.

The first Pharmacy Council of India was constituted in 1949. Its constitution and functions are discussed below.

(A) Constitution : Pharmacy Council of India is constituted after every five years with the following members included in it

1. Six persons elected by UGC from amongst the teaching staff of a College or a University, granting a degree or diploma in pharmacy.

   Amongst these at least one teacher of pharmacy, pharmacognosy, pharmaceutical chemistry and pharmacology must be included.

2. Six persons are nominated by the Central Government and they should be angaged in the practice of pharmacy or pharmaceutical chemistry. Four of them should possess degree or diploma in pharmacy.

3. One person; elected by the Medical Council of India out of its members.

4. One persons is nominated by the Governments of each state, who should be a registered pharmacist. Each Union Territory after five years of the commencement of Pharmacy Amendment Act 1976 shall also nominate one person eligible for registration as a pharmacist.

5. One person, elected by each of the State Pharmacy Council from amongst its members who should be a registered pharmacist.

   After chapter II of the Act comes into force, each of the states of Karela, Mysore and Rajasthan would nominate a person eligible for registration as a pharmacist after 5 years.

6. A representative of U.G.C. and a representative of A.I.C.T.E.

7. Following are the ex-officio members
   (a) Director General Health Services
   (b) Director Central Drugs Laboratory
   (c) The Drugs Controller of India.

Apart from the above mentioned elected, nominated and ex-officio members; a President, a Vice-president and five other members constitute the Executive Committee of the Council:

— The council may also appoint a secretary who may

also act as its Registrar and its treasurer and other such officers and servants as per the requirement to carry out its functions and duties.

— Council is deemed to be a corporate body, having a perpetual succession and a common seal with the power to aquire and hold movable and immovable property.

— Elected and nominated members hold office for period of 5 years.

— All the members are eligible for re-election and re-nomination.

— A member would deemed to have vacated his seat if he does not attend three consecutive meetings of council without sufficient reason.

— Persons nominated by U.G.C. or Medical Council of India or state Pharmacy Council of India is no longer the member of teaching staff of University, or Medical Council of India or ceases to be registered pharmacist shall also cease to be the member of Pharmacy Council of India.

FUNCTIONS

Pharmacy Council of India is entrusted with following functions :

(1) Education Regulation

(2) Approval/Withdrawal of Approvals of Insttutions

(3) Approval of Other Qualifications

(4) Maintenance of Central Register of Pharmacists.

(1) Education Regulations : Education Regulations are laid down by the Pharmacy Council of India with the approval of Government of India and after circulating the draft to each state Government and after duly considering their comments, if any. The effectiveness of the Regulations is monitored by the Council from time to time. Necessary amendments may be recommended by the Council. It includes

— Minimum qualification required for admission to the

course and duration of training as well as course to be covered.

- Nature of practical training to be undertaken after completion of the regular course which should not be less than 750 hrs to be covered in three months in a recognised hospital/dispensary/pharmacy or chemist or druggist shop.
- It lays down the minimum facilities equipment to be provided to students for running the course in an Institution.
- Requirements to be fulfilled by the hospitals, institutions etc. providing the practical training after completion of regular course.
- Requirements to be fulfilled by the authorities holding approved examinations.

(2) Approval/Withdrawal of Approval of Institutions: For getting the approval from PCI, an institution interested in conducting the course or holding an examination for the pharmacists.

(i) Approval : For the purpose Council deputes its inspectors to visit these institutions and see whether the institution has the prescribed facilities for

(a) running a course

(b) holding an examination in accordance with the Education Regulations should apply to PCI in the prescribed format.

Inspector reports to Council on the sufficiency of facilities, standard of examinations conducted. Ultimately on the report of inspectors of the Council is satisfied that the course/examination is in accordance with the Education Regulations, the said course shall deemed to be approved for qualifying for registration as a pharmacist under the Act.

A resolution passed at a meeting of the Council would make the declaration of approval. It should also be published in the official gazette.

(ii) Withdrawl of approval : Pharmacy Council of India may disapprove a course after giving notice to the institution or authority concerned if it comes to its notice that the course of study or examination conducted does not continue to be in the conformity with ER.

Sometimes approval may be given conditionally subject to the fulfillment of the conditions mentioned by the PCI.

(3) Recognition of other qualification : The Council can recognise any other qualification granted by the authority outside India provided it guarantees the requisite technical skill and knowledge which is sufficient for registration as a pharmacist under the Act.

— For registration normally the citizens of India holding such qualification will be eligible.

— Citizens of other countries holding the requisite qualification shall be eligible only if Indian national holding the same qualification is allowed to enter the profession of pharmacy in that country.

(4) Maintenance of Central Register of Pharmacist : PCI is required to maintain a Register called Central Register which contains the names of all persons registered as pharmacist in different states under the provisions of the Act.

— It is published in the Gazette of India and has to be revised suitably from time to time within the meaning of Indian Evidence Act 1872.

— It is deemed to be a public document.

— PCI should be supplied five copies of Registers by the State Pharmacy Council after 1st April of each year.

STATE PHARMACY COUNCILS AND JOINT STATE PHARMACY COUNCILS

State Pharmacy Councils and Joint State Pharmacy Councils are constituted under the Act by the State Governments.

— State Pharmacy Council is constituted by a single state.

— Joint State Pharmacy Councils are formed when two or more states enter into an agreement in which one state agrees to serve the needs of other participating states. Such agreement may provide for the

1. Division of expenditure between the participating states.
2. Consultation between the participating State Governments with reference to the matters arising under the Act.
3. It may make incidental and ancillary provisions, as may be necessary for giving effect to the agreement under the Act.

Constitution of State Pharmacy Council and Joint State Pharmacy Council.

State Pharmacy Council	Joint State Pharmacy Council
Elected Member	
(1) Six registered pharmacists elected from amongst themselves	3-5 registered pharmacists elected amongst themselves
(2) One member elected by Medical Council of the state out of its members	One person elected by Medical Council of each of the participating states from amongst its members
Nominated Members	
(1) 5 persons (at least three should possess diploma or degree in pharmacy, pharmaceutical chemistry or be a registered pharmacist) nominated by State Government	2-4 members nominated by each of the participating states out of which half should possess degree or diploma in pharmacy or be a registered Pharmacist
Ex-officio Members	
(1) Chief Administrative medical officer of the state	Cheif Administrative Medical Officer of each of the

	participating states
(2) Officer in charge of drug control organisation of the state	Officer in charge of the drug control organisation of participating state
(3) Government analyst under Drugs and Cosmetic Act as the State Government may appoint on this behalf	Government analyst of each of the participating State

Each State Council shall have a president and a vice-president who are elected by the members from amongst themselves provided that for years from the first constitution of the council, the president will be nominated by the State Government.

FOLLOWING POINTS SHOULD BE NOTED

— President or vice-president holds the office for upto 5 years.

— He is eligible for re-election.

— Any member can resign at any time by writing to the President.

— If any member is absent in three consecutive meetings without sufficient cause, his seat is deemed to be vacated.

— A casual vacancy in the State Council can be filled by fresh nomination/election.

— Any member of State Council is eligible for re-nomination or re-election.

— State Council may appoint a Registrar who may act as its secretary and also as treasurer.

Functions of State Pharmacy Council

(1) Inspection

(2) Registration of Pharmacist

INSPECTION

State Council may appoint inspectors having the prescribed qualifications. Inspectors are required to perform the following functions.

- Inspect the premises where drugs are compounded or dispensed.
- Investigate about the complaints made in writing regarding the contravention of Act.
- To see whether persons engaged in the compounding or dispensing of medicines are only registered pharmacists.
- To institute the prosecution when directed by the Executive Committee of the State Pharmacy Council.

Inspector is deemed to be a public servant as defined under Indian Penal Code (Section 21) and any person obstructing an inspector in exercising his powers is punishable with imprisonment upto six months or fine of Rs 1000 or both.

REGISTRATION OF PHARMACIST

Names of the registered pharmacists are entered in the registers which are maintained by the Central Council and State Pharmacy Councils. Pharmacy Act provides for the registration of Pharmacist, having the prescribed qualification to regulate the entry of persons in the field of this profession.

The register contains the full particulars about the name of pharmacist, residential address of registered pharmacist, date of admission to first register, details of qualifications, professional address in case of employed personnel. Two types of registers made by State Council are

(1) First Register

(2) Subsequent Register.

(1) First Register : For the entry of name in the first register a tribunal of three persons and a registrar is appointed by notification in the official Gazette. A date is appointed by the State Government, before which the applications along with the prescribed fee must reach the tribunal. After going through the applications registrar enters the names of persons qualified for registration. Every person whose name is entered in the register gets a certificate issued by the registrar which is later on handed over to State Council after its constitution.

(2) Subsequent Register : Subsequent register is maintained by the State Government for the registration of persons having the specified qualifications before the Education Regulations have taken effect in the State. After the Education Regulation becomes effective in the State, a person is entitled for registration

— if he has attained the age of 18 years;

— resides/carries business of pharmacy in the State;

— has passed approved examination;

— possess a qualification granted by authority outside India which is approved by Central Council;

— or a person is registered pharmacist in another state.

GENERAL QUALIFICATIONS SPECIFIED FOR REGISTRATION ARE FOLLOWING

— has passed an examination recognised as adequate by the State Government for compounders or dispensers

— has been engaged in the compounding of drugs in the hospital or dispensary or any other place where drugs are regularly dispensed on prescriptions of RMPs, for a period not less than five years

— holds a degree of an Indian University other than degree or diploma in pharmacy or pharm chemistry and has been engaged in the compounding of drugs in hospital or dispensary or other place where drugs are regularly dispensed on prescription of medical practitioners for a period of not less than three years

4. For subsequent registration the person should satisfy the conditions prescribed and approved by Central Council or possess a qualification granted by an authority

outside India, but approved by Central Council and has passed a matriculation or equivalent examination granted by an authority outside India which is approved by Central Council.

SPECIAL PROVISIONS FOR REGISTRATION OF CERTAIN PERSONS

The Pharmacy (Amendment) Act of 1959, made special provisions for registration of the following persons like

(a) Displaced persons who had been engaged in the business or profession of pharmacy as their principal means of livelihood before the 4th March 1946 the conditions for registration in the first registers of the states.

(b) Citizens of India who had been engaged in the business or profession of pharmacy abroad and satisfied the conditions for registration in the first registers of the states.

(c) have been engaged in the compounding of drugs in hospital or dispencery or other place in which drugs are regularly dispensed on prescriptions of medical practitioners after a total period of not less than five years prior to the date appointed.

REGISTRATION OF DISPLACED PERSONS

Repatriates and other persons.

The Pharmacy (Amendment) Act, 1976 provided for the registration of the certain categories of persons for a period of two years from the commencement of this Amendment Act like.

(a) Persons who possess degree or diploma in pharmacy or pharmaceutical chemistry or chemists and druggists' diploma of an Indian university or State Government, or have passed an examination recognised adequate for compounders and dispensers by the State Government and who are eligible for registration between the closing of the first register and the date when the Education Regulations came into effect.

(b) Persons approved as "qualified persons" before 31st December 1969 for compounding & dispensing of medicines under the Drugs & Cosmetics Act 1940 & Rules.

(c) "displaced persons" from Bangladesh who left that country after 14th April 1957 but before 25th March 1971 and "repatriates" from Burma, Srilanka, Uganda or any other country who left or were displaced from such countries between 14th April 1957 & 25th March 1971 and were carrying business or profession of pharmacy as the principal means of their livelihood for a total period of five years prior to the date of application.

REMOVAL OF NAMES FROM REGISTER

The Executive Committee of a State Council may order that the name of a registered pharmacist shall be removed from the register on the following grounds :

(a) If his name has been entered in the Register by error or an account of misrepresentation or suppression of a material fact, or

(b) If he has been convicted of any offence or has been found guilty of any Infamous conduct in any professional respect which in the opinion of the Executive Committee renders him unfit to be kept in the register.

(c) If a person in his employment in connection with any business of pharmacy has been convicted of any such offence or has been found guilty of any such infamous conduct as would. If such person himself was a registered pharmacist, renders him liable to have his name removed from the register.

An order for removal of name from the register may direct that the person whose name is removed shall be ineligible for registration in the state under this Act either permanently or for any specified period of time. The order is subject to confirmation by the State Council and does not take effect until the expiry of three months from the date of such confirmation.

This is justified so that a person whose name has been removed from the register may search for an alternate means of livelihood within three months.

PRINTING OF REGISTERS

Subsequent to the commencement of the pharmacy (Amendment) Act 1959, as soon as may be after the 1st April, every year the registrars of the State Council were required to print the registers as they stood on the date. They are also required to print the registers as they stood on that date. They are also requird to print as soon as may be after the 1st April in each year, copies of the annual supplement to the register, showing all additions to, and other amendments in, the said register. The register should bring up to-date the respective registers three months before ordinary elections of the State Council are held and print copies of the register.

PENALTIES UNDER THE ACT

(1) Penalty For falsely claiming to be registered pharmacist: Any person who falsely claims to be registered pharmacist and uses in connection with his name or title any words or letters reasonably calculated to suggest that he is a registered pharmacist shall be punished on first conviction with fine extending upto Rs 500 and on any subsequent conviction with imprisonment upto 6 months or with fine not exceeding Rs 1000 or with both.

(2) Penalty For dispensing by unregistered persons : On or after the date notified by the State Govt. in this behalf, no person other than a registered pharmacist can compound prepare, mix, or dispense any medicine on the prescription of a medical practitioner. This however does not apply to dispensing of medicines by a medical practitioner to his patients.

(3) Penalty for failing to surrender certificate of registration: If any person whose name has been removed from the register fails without sufficient cause to surrender his certificate of registration, he shall be punishable with fine extending to Rs 50.

4

DRUGS AND COSMETICS ACT

Drugs are vital social instruments for the prevention and cure of diseases and ailments of different nature. The drugs have a dubious past with most of them having superstitious and magic cure. But in the current century establishing themselves on scientific lines and reduce the morality ratios and increase life span. In India it is stated that the average life rate was just 27 years during the last half a century which has risen to 60 years or so. It is now seen that the drugs have played a very important role in the health of human beings and it calls for a careful controls over their production and standardisation, use etc.

It is stated that till 1940 the country had no rules and laws whatsoever in regard to manufacture, composition and sale etc. of drugs. The first Act of enacting this Drugs Act was enforced in 1940. This Act was required to control over operations in respect of allopathic drugs only. Since then this Act has been amended several times which included under its purview Ayurvedic, Unani, Siddha and Homoeopathic drugs as well as cosmetics. The "allopathic drug" includes all substances, other than food, intended to affect the structure on other functions of human body including contraceptions and all substances, used for the destruction of insects and notified in this regard by the Central Government, which cause diseases in human beings or animals are also deemed to be drugs for purposes of this Act.

A number of provisions of the Act related to import, manufacture and sale of allopathic drugs together with the provision for related matters like labelling and administration etc. are discussed in the sections to follow. Provisions of the Act are applicable to drugs used under other systems like Ayurvedic, Homoeopathic etc. as well as to cosmetics are elaborated later in separate sections.

Due to increased consumption of cosmetics in the country and prolonged contact with the skin which could cause dermatitis and cumulative toxicities thus affecting the health, the control envisaged over drugs have been extended to cosmetics too. This Act extends to whole of India and in this Act.

Important Definitions Under the Act

"DRUG" INCLUDES

(i) all medicines for internal or external use of human beings or animals and all substances intended to be used for or in the diagnosis, treatment, mitigation or prevention of any disease or disorder in human beings or animals including preparation applied on human body for the purpose of repelling insects like mosquitoes.

(ii) such substances (other than food) intended to affect the structure of any function of the human body or intended to be used for the destruction of insects which cause disease in human beings or animals as may be specified from time to time by the Central Government by notification in official Gazette.

(iii) all substances intended for use as components of a drug including empty gelatin capsules and

(iv) such devices intended for internal or external use in the diagnosis, treatment, mitigation or prevention of disease or disorder in human beings or animals, as may be specified from time to time by Central Government by notification in official gazette.

Ayurvedic, Siddha or Unani drugs include—all medicines intended for internal or external use for or in the diagnosis, treatment, mitigation or prevention of disease or disorder in human beings or animals and manufactured exclusively in accordance with the formulae described in the authoritative books of Ayurvedic, Siddha and Unani Tibb systems of medicine, specified in the first Schedule.

The Board Means

(i) in relation to Ayurvedic, Siddha or Unani drug the Ayurvedic, Siddha and Unani drug Technical Advisory Board constituted under Section 33 C and

(ii) in relation to any other drug or cosmetic the Drugs Technical Advisory Board constituted under Section 5.

Cosmetic means—any article intended to be rubbed, poured, sprinkled or sprayed on or introduced into or otherwise applied to human body or any part thereof for cleansing, beautifying, promoting attractiveness or altering the appearance and includes any article intended for use as a component of cosmetic which does not include soap.

Manufacture—in relation to any drug or cosmetic includes any process or part of process for making, altering, ornamenting, finishing, packing, labelling, breaking up or otherwise treating or adopting any drug or cosmetic with a view to its sale or distribution but does not include the compounding or dispensing of any drug or the packing of any drug or cosmetic.

PATENT OR PROPRIETARY MEDICINE MEANS

(i) in relation to Ayurvedic, Siddha or Unani Tibb systems of medicine all formulations containing only such ingredients mentioned in the formulae described in the authoriatative books of Ayurveda, Siddha or Unani Tibb systems of medicine specified in the first schedule but does not include a medicine which is administered by parentral route and also a formulation included in the authoritative books.

(ii) in relation to any other systems of medicine, a drug which is a remedy or prescription presented in a form ready for internal or external administration of human beings or animals and which is not included in the edition of Indian Pharmacopoeia or any other pharmacopoeia authorised in this behalf by Central Government.

Drugs Technical Advisory Board

Drugs technical advisory board is constituted under the Act to advise the Central Government and the State Government on technical matters arising out of the administration of this Act.

Central Drugs Laboratory

Central Drugs Laboratory after consultation with the Board helps to check over the standards of drugs and cosmetics by taking random samples manufactured or offered for sale and getting them tested and analysed either in drugs control laboratories in the states or in the Central Drugs Laboratory. Regular control over manufacture and sale is governed by periodical inspection of the licensed premises by Drug Inspectors, who are specially appointed for the purpose under the Act.

Drugs Consultative Committee

The Central Government constitute on advisory committee to be called "the Drug Consultative Committee" to advise the Central Government, the State Governments and the Drugs Technical Advisory Board on any matter tending to secure uniformity throughout India in the administration of the Act.

The various schedules in the Act are—

Schedule A : It includes all forms (nearly 40) for the application for licence to import, manufacture of various categories of drug, their renewal, certificate of test or analysis by Central Drugs Laboratory, application forms for loan licence, repack licence, licence to sell, stock, exhibit and applications for approval for carrying out tests on drugs/cosmetics or raw materials etc.

Schedule B : Fees for test or analysis by the Central Drugs Laboratory or the Government Analysis.

Schedule C : Biological and special products.

(I) : Other Special products.

Schedule D : Class of drugs : Extent and conditions of exemption.

Schedule E : List of Poisonous substances (omitted) w.e.f. 22.6.82.

(I) : List of poisonous substances under the Ayurvedic (including Siddha and Unani systems of medicine.

Schedule F : Related to production of vaccines, and provisions applicable to particular. Sera and antitoxin which is omitted.

(I) : Provisions applicable to production of bacterial vaccines, viral vaccines, all sera from living animals, standardisation and manufacture of diagnostic agents.

(II) : Standards for Surgical Dressings.

(III) : Standards for Umbilical tapes.

(IV) : Standards for opthalamic preparations.

Schedule G : List of drugs for which caution should be written on the lable that it is dangerous to take preparation except under medical supervision.

Schedule H : Prescription drugs.

Schedule I : Particulars as to proportion of poison in certain cases (omitted).

Schedule J : Diseases and ailments (by whatever name described) which a drug may not purport to prevent or cure.

Schedule K : Class of drugs; Extent and conditions of exemption.

Schedule L : Omitted.

Schedule M : Good manufacturing practices and requirements of premises, plant and equipment.

(I) : Requirements of factory premises for manufacture of Homoeopathic preparation.

(II) : Requirement of factory premises for manufacture of cosmetics.

(III) : Requirement of factory premises for manufacture of medical devices.

Schedule N : List of minimum equipment for the efficient running of a pharmacy.

Schedule O : Standard for disinfectant fluid.

Schedule P : Life period of drugs.

(I) : Pack size of drugs.

Schedule Q : List of colours permitted in cosmetics and soaps.

Schedule R : Condoms.

(I) : Standards for medical devices.

Schedule S : Standards for cosmetics.

Schedule T : Requirements of factory premises and hygienic conditions.

Schedule U : Particulars to be shown in manufacturing records.

Schedule V : Standards for patent or proprietary medicines.

Schedule W : Names of the drugs which shall be marketed under generic names only.

Schedule X : List of drugs for the import requiring special licences for their manufacture, Sale etc.

Schedule Y : Requirements and Guidelines on clinical trials for import and manufacture of new drugs.

For the purpose of import, the material brought from a place other than India to a place in India, the drugs are classified as below:

(i) Drug whose import is prohibited.

(ii) Drugs which may be imported under licence or permit.

(iii) Drugs which can be imported without obtaining licence.

Misbranded drugs : For the purpose of this chapter a drug shall deemed to be misbranded—

(a) if it is so coloured, coated, powdered or polished that damage is concealed or if it is made to appear of better or greater therapeutic value than it really is or

(b) if it is not labelled in the prescribed manner or

(c) if its label or container or anything accompanying the drug bears any statement, design or device which makes any false claim for the drug or which is false or misleading in any particular.

Adulterated drugs : A drug shall deemed to be adulterated.

(a) if it consists, in whole or in part of any filthy, putrid or decomposed substance or

(b) if it has been prepared, packed or stored under insanitary conditions whereby it may have been contaminated with filth or whereby it may have been rendered injurious to health or

(c) if its container is composed in whole or in part of any poisonous or deleterious substance which may render the contents injurious to health or

(d) if it bears or contains, for purpose of colouring only, a colour other than which is prescribed or

(e) if it contains any harmful or toxic substance

which may render it injurious to health or (f) if any substance has been mixed therewith so as to reduce its quality or strength.

Spurious drugs : A drug shall deemed to be spurious

(a) if it is imported under a name which belongs to another drug.

(b) if it is imitation or is a substitute for another drug or resembles another drug in a manner likely to deceive or bears upon it or upon its lable or container the name of another drug unless it is plainly and conspicuously marked so as to reveal its true character and its lack of identity with such other drugs or

(c) if the label or container bears the name of an individual or company purporting to be the manufacturer of the drug which individual or company is fictitious or does not exist or

(d) if it has been substituted wholly or in part by another drug or substance of (e) if it purports to be the product of a manufacturer of whom it is not truly a product.

Spurious Cosmetics : Same as spurious drugs so read 'cosmetics' instead of 'drugs'.

Misbranded Cosmetics : A cosmetic shall be deemed to be misbranded—

(a) if it contains a colour which is not prescribed or

(b) if it is not labelled in the prescribed manner or

(c) if the label or container or anything accompanying the cosmetic bears any statement which is false or misleading in any particular.

MANUFACTURE, SALE AND DISTRIBUTION OF DRUGS AND COSMETICS

Prohibition of manufacture and sale of certain drugs and cosmetics: No person shall himself or by any other person on this behalf—

(a) Manufacture for sale or for distribution or sell or stock or exhibit or offer for sale or distribute—

(i) any drug or cosmetic which is not of a standard quality or is misbranded, adulterated or spurious

(ii) Any patent or proprietary medicine whose formula is not disclosed.

(iii) Drugs which claim to prevent or cure any of the diseases or ailments specified in schedule J to the Rules.

(iv) Any cosmetic containing any igredient which may render it unsafe or harmful for use under the directions indicated or recommended.

(v) Any drug or cosmetic in contravention of any of the provisions of this act or any rule made thereunder.

(b) Sell or stock or exhibit or offer for sale or distribute any drug or cosmetic which has been imported or manufactured in contravention of provisions of the Act.

(c) Manufacture for sale or for distribution or sell or stock or exhibit or offer for sale or distribute any drug or cosmetic except under and in accordance with the conditions of a licence issued for such purpose.

Any person not being the manufacturer of a drug or cosmetic or his agent for the distribution there of has to disclose the name of the person from whom he acquired the drug or cosmetic.

STANDARDS TO BE COMPLIED WITH BY IMPORTED DRUGS AND BY DRUGS MANUFACTURED FOR SALE, STOCKED OR EXHIBITION FOR SALE OR DISTRIBUTED

Class of drug	*Standard to be complied with*
1. Patent or proprietary medicines (other than Homoeopathic medicines).	The formula or list of ingredients displayed in the prescribed manner on the label or container and such other standards as may be prescribed.
2. (Substances commonly known as vaccines, sera, toxins, toxoids, antitoxins and antigens and biolo-	The standards maintained at the International Laboratory for Biological Standards, standard Serum Ins-

	gical products of like nature, for human use or for veterinary use.	titute, Copenhagen, and at the Central Veterinary Laboratory, Weybridge, Surrey, U.K., and such other laboratories recognised by the World Health Organisation from time to time, and such further standards of strength, quality, and purity, as may be prescribed]
3.	Substances (othe than food) intended to affect the structure or any function of the human body or intended to be used for the destruction of vermin or insects which cause disease in human beings or animals.	Such standards as may be prescribed.
4.	Homoeopathic medicines:	
(a)	Drugs included in the Homoeopathic Pharmacopoeia of India.	Standards of identity, purity and strength specified in the edition of the Homoeopathic Pharmacopoeia of India for the time being and such other standards as may be prescribed.
(b)	Drugs not included in the Homoeopathic Pharmacopoeia of India but which are included in the Homoeopathic Pharmacopoeia of the United States of America or the United Kingdom or the German Homoeopathic Pharmacopoeia.	Standards of identity, purity and strength prescribed for the drugs in the edition of such Pharmacopoeia for the time being in which they are given and such other standards as may be prescribed.
(c)	Drugs not included in the Homoeopathic Pharmacopoeia of India or the United States of America, or the United Kingdom or the German Homoeopathic Pharmacopoeia.	The formula or list of ingredients displayed in the prescribed manner on the label of the container and such other standards as may be prescribed by the Central Government.
5.	Other drugs:	
(a)	Drugs included in the Indian Pharmacopoeia.	Standards of identity, purity and strength specified in the edition of the Indian Pharmacopoeia for the time being in force and such other standards as may be prescribed. In case the standards of identity, purity and strength for drugs are not specified in the edition of the Indian Pharmacopoeia for the time being in force but are specified in

	the edition of the Indian Pharmacopoeia immediately preceding, the standards of identity, purity and strength shall be those occurring in such immediately preceding edition of the Indian Pharmacopoeia and such other standards as may be prescribed.
(b) Drugs not included in the Indian Pharmacopoeia but which are included in the official Pharmacopoeia of any other country.	Standards of identity, purity and strength specified for drugs in the edition of such official Pharmacopoeia of any other country for the time being in force and such other standards as may be prescribed. In case the standards of identity, purity and strength for drugs are not specified in the edition of such official Pharmacopoeia for the time being in force, but are specified in the edition immediately preceding, the standards of identity, purity and strength shall be those occurring in such immediately preceding edition of such official Pharmacopoeia and such other standards as may be prescribed.

If drugs are manufactured on more than one set of premises a separate application shall be made and a separate licence shall be issued in respect of each such set of premises.

GRANT OR RENEWAL OF LICENCES BY THE CENTRAL LICENCE APPROVING AUTHORITY

Licences for the manufacture and removal are issued by central licence approving authority appointed by the Central Government on receipt of the application for the same. Only if they are satisfied that the applicant is in a position to fulfill the requirements laid down in the rule. The following categories of licences are issued—

(1) Licence for manufacture of drugs other than those specified in Schedule C and C(I).

(2) Licence for manufacture of Schedule C and C(I) drugs.

(3) Licence for manufacture of drugs meant for ex-

amination, test or analysis.

(4) Loan Licence.

(5) Repacking Licence.

On receipt of the application in the prescribed format along with the fees the inspectors appointed by the Central Government, inspect the premises, with or without an expert in the concerned field. If the applicant fulfills all requirements than within three months licence is issued. If an applicant changed the premises the licence is valid only upto three months and thereafter fresh licence is required.

'Repacking' means the process of breaking up any drug from a bulk container into small packages and the labelling of each such package with a view to its sale and distribution but does not include the compounding or dispensing or the packing of any drug in the ordinary course of the retail business.

Conditions for the grant or renewal of licence for the manufacture of Schedule C & C(I) drugs and Schedule X drugs—Before a licence is granted following conditions shall be complied with by the applicant—

(1) the manufacture shall be conducted under the active direction and personal supervision of competent technical staff consisting at least of one person who is a whole-time employee and who is—

(i) a graduate in Pharmacy or Pharmaceutical Chemistry of [a University established in India by law or has an equivalent qualification recognised and notified by the Central Government for such purpose] and has had at least [eighteen months' practical experience] after the graduation in the manufacture of drugs. This period of experience may, however, be reduced by six months if the person has undergone training in manufacture of drugs for a period of six months during his University course; or

(ii) a graduate in Science of [a University established in India by law or has an equivalent qualification recognised and notified by the Central Government for such purpose] who for the purpose of his degree has studied Chemistry as a principal subject and has had at least three years' practical experience in the manufacture of drugs after his graduation; or

(iii) a graduate in Chemical Engineering or Chemical Technology or Medicine of [a University established in India by law or has an equivalent qualification recognised and notified by the Central Government for such purpose] with general training and practical experience, extending over a period of not less than three years in the manufacture of drugs, after his graduation; or

(iv) holding any foreign qualification the quality and content of training of which are comparable with those prescribed in clause (a), clause (b) or clause (c) and is permitted to work as competent technical staff under this rule by the Central Government:]

Provided that any person who was immediately before the 29th June, 1957, actively directing and personally supervising the manufacture of drugs and whose name was accordingly entered in any licence granted in Form 25 [or Form 25-F] as it existed before that date shall be deemed to be qualified for the purposes of this rule:

Provided further that the Licensing Authority may, in the matter of manufacture of disinfectant fluids, insecticides, liquid paraffin, medicinal gases, non-chemical contraceptives, plaster of Paris and surgical dressings, for the manufacture of which the knowledge of Pharmaceutical Chemistry or Pharmacy is not essential, permit the manufacture of the substance under the active direction and personal supervision of the competent technical staff, who, although not having any of the qualifications included in clauses (a), (b) or (c) of this rule, has, in the opinion of the Licensing Authority, adequate experience in the manufacture of such substance.]

(2) The factory premises shall comply with the conditions prescribed in Schedule M.

(3) The applicant shall provide adequate space, plant and equipment for the manufacturing operations; the space, plant and equipment recommended for various operations are given in Schedule M.

(4) The applicant shall provide and maintain adequate staff, premises and laboratory equipment for carrying out tests of the strength, quality and purity of the substances at the testing unit, which shall be separate from the manufacturing unit and head of the testing unit shall be independent of the head of the manufacturing unit:

Provided that the manufacturing units, which before the commencement of the Drugs and Cosmetics (Amendment) Rules, 1977, were making arrangements with institutions approved by the licensing authority for such tests to be carried out on their behalf may continue such arrangements up to the 30th June, 1977:

Provided further that for tests requiring sophisticated instrumentation techniques or biological or microbiological methods other than sterility the licensing authority may permit such tests to be conducted by institutions approved by it [under Part XV(A) of these Rules] for this purpose.]

(i) The head of the testing unit referred to in condition (4) shall possess a degree in Medicine or Science or Pharmacy or Pharmaceutical Chemistry of a University recognised for this purpose and shall have experience in the testing of drugs, which in the opinion of the licensing authority is considered adequate.

(5) The applicant shall make adequate arrangements for the storage of drugs manufactured by him.

(6) The applicant shall, while applying for a licence to manufacture patent or proprietary medicines, furnish to the Licencing Authority evidence and data justifying that the patent or proprietary medicines—

(i) contain the constituent ingredients in therapeutic/prophylactic quantities as determined in relation to the claims or conditions for which the medicines are recommended for use or claimed to be useful;

(ii) are safe for use in the context of the vehicles, excipients additives and pharmaceutical aids used in the formulation and under the conditions in which the formulations for administration and use are recommended;

(iii) are stable under the conditions of storage recommended; and

(iv) contain such ingredients and in such quantities for which there is therapeutic justification.

(7) The licensee shall comply with the requirements of good manufacturing practices as laid down in Schedule M.

Conditions for the grant or renewal of licence for repacking of drugs other than Schedule C and C(I) and Schedule X.—Following conditions shall be complied by the applicant—

(i) The repacking operation shall be carried out under hygienic conditions and under the supervision of a competent person.

(ii) The factory premises shall comply with the conditions prescribed in Schedule M.

(iii) The applicant shall have adequate arrangements in his own premises for carrying out test for the strength, quality and purity of the drugs at a testing unit which shall be separate from the repacking unit.

Conditions for the grant or renewal of loan licence for drugs other than Schedule C and C(I) and Schedule X.— The applicant should submit sufficient data justifying that the patent or proprietary medicine—

(i) contain the constituent ingredients in therapeutic/prophylactic quantities as determined in relation to the claims or conditions for which the medicines are recommended for use or claimed to be useful.

(ii) are safe for use in the context of the vehicles, excipients, additives and pharmaceutical aids used in the formulations for administration and use are rcommended.

(iii) are stable under the conditions of storage recommended and

(iv) contain such ingredients and in such quantities for which there is therapeutic justification.

Duration of licence: An original licence, renewed licence or loan licence unless sooner suspended or cancelled is valid upto 31st December of the year following the year in which it is granted or renewed, the application for the renewal of a licence is made before its expiry or if the application is made within six months of its expiry.

Conditions of licence for manufacturing drugs specified in Schedule 'X'—A licence issued shall be subject to the conditions stated earlier and to the following further conditions, namely—

(a) the licensee shall provide and maintain staff, premises and the equipment as specified;

(b) the licensee shall comply with the provisions of the Act and of these rules and with such further requirements, if any, as may be specified in any rules subsequently made under Chapter IV of the Act, provided that where such further requirements are specified in the rules, these would come into force, four months after publication in the official Gazette;

(c) the licensee shall either in his own laboratory or in any other laboratory approved by the licensing authority (under Part XV(A) of these Rules) test each batch or lot of the raw material used by him for the manufacture of his products and also each batch of the final product and shall maintain records or registers showing the particulars in respect of such tests as specified in Schedule U. The records or registers shall be retained for a period of 5 years from the date of manufacture;

(d) the licensee shall keep records of the details of manufacture as per particulars given in Schedule U of each batch of the drugs manufactured by him and such records shall be retained for a period of five years;

(e) the licensee shall allow an (Inspectors authorised by the Act) to enter, with or without prior notice, any premises and to inspect the plant and the process of manufacture and the means employed in standardising and testing the drugs;

(f) the licensee shall allow an (Inspector authorised by the Act) to inspect all registers and records maintained under these rules and to take samples of the manufactured drugs and shall supply to such Inspectors such information as he may require for the purpose of ascertaining whether the provisions of the Act and the rules thereunder have been observed;

(g) the licensee shall, from time to time, report to the licensing authority any changes in the expert staff responsible for the manufacture or testing of the drugs and any material alterations in the premises or plant used for the purpose which have been made since the date of the last inspection made on behalf of the licensing authority;

(h) the licensee shall, on request, furnish to the licensing authority, the controlling authority or to such authorities as the licensing authority or the controlling authority may direct, from every batch or batches of drugs as the licensing authority or the controlling authority may from time to time specify, a sample of such quantity as may be considered adequate by such authority for any examination and, if so required, also furnish full protocols of tests which have been applied;

(i) if the licensing authority (for the controlling authority) so directs and if requested by the licensee who has also furnished prima facie reasons for such directions, the licensee shall not sell or offer for sale any batch in respect of which a sample is or protocols are furnished under claused (h) until a certificate authorising the sale of the batch has been issued to him by or on behalf of the licensing authority (or the controlling authority);

(j) the licensee shall on being informed by the licensing authority (or the controlling authority) that any part of any batch of the drug has been found by the licensing authority (or the controlling authority) not to conform with the standards of strength, quality or purity specified in these rules and on being directed so to do, withdraw the remainder of the batch from sale, and, so far as may in the particular circumstances of the case be practicable, recall all issues already made from that batch;

(k) the licensee shall maintain an Inspection Book in Form 35 to enable an Inspector to record his impressions and the defects noticed;)

(l) the licensee shall maintain reference samples from each batch of the drugs manufactured by him in a quantity which is at least twice the quantity of the drug required to conduct all the tests performed on the batch. In case of drugs bearing an expiry date on the label, the reference samples shall be maintained for a period of three months beyond the date of expiry of potency. In case of drugs where no date of expiry of potency is specified on the label, the referenc samples shall be maintained for a period of three years from the date of manufacture;

(m) the licensee, who has been granted a licence in Form 25-F, shall :

(i) forward to the licensing authority of the concerned States of manufacture and supply of the drug a statement of the sales effected to the manufacturers, wholesalers, retailers, hospitals, dispensaries and nursing homes and Registered Medical Practitioners every three months;

(ii) maintain accounts of all transactions giving details as indicated below in a register bound and serially page numbered and such records shall be retained for a period of five years or one year after the expiry of potency, whichever is later:

A. Accounts of the drugs specified in Schedule X used for the manufacture:

1. Date of issue.
2. Name of the drug.
3. Opening balance of stock on the production day.
4. Quantity received, if any, and source from where received.
5. Quantity used in manufacture.
6. Balance quantity on hand at the end of the production day.
7. Signature of the person incharge.

B. Accounts of production:

1. Date of manufacture.
2. Name of the drug.
3. Batch Number.
4. Quantity of raw material used in manufacture.
5. Anticipated yield.
6. Actual yield.
7. Wastage.
8. Quantity of the manufactured goods transferred.

C. Accounts of the manufactured drugs:

1. Date of manufacture.
2. Name of the drug.
3. Batch Number.
4. Opening Balance.
5. Quantity manufactured.
6. Quantity sold.
7. Name of the purchaser and his address.
8. Balance quantity at the end of the day.
9. Signature of the person incharge.

(n) The licensee shall store drugs specified in Schedule X in bulk form and when any of such drug is required for manufacture in a place other than its place of storage it shall be kept in a separate place under the direct custody of a responsible person.]

(o) The licensee shall comply, with the requirements of 'God Manufacturing Practices' as laid down in Schedule M.]

Loan Licences: Loan licence means a licence which a licencing authority may issue to an applicant who does not have his own arrangements for manufacture but who intends to avail himself to the manufacturing facilities owned by licensee.

The licensing authority satisfy itself that the manufacturing unit has adequate equipment, staff, capacity for manufacture and facilities to undertake the manufacture on behalf of the applicant for a loan licence.

Conditions for Issue of Loan Licence

Loan licence to manufacture drugs specified in Schedule C and C(I) and Schedule X :

(1) The licence shall be deemed to be cancelled or suspended if the licence owned by the licensee whose manufacturing facilities have been availed of by the licensee is cancelled or suspended as the case may be under the rules.

(2) The licensee shall comply with the provisions of the Act.

(3) The licensee shall test each batch or lot of the raw material used by him for the manufacture of his products and also each batch of the final product and shall maintain records or register showing the particulars in respect of such tests as specified in Schedule U. The records or registers shall be retained for a period of five years from the date of manufacture. The licensee shall allow an inspector to inspect all registers and records maintained under these rules and shall supply to the inspector such information as he may require for the purpose of ascertaining the provisions of the Act.

(4) The licensee shall either :

   (i) Provide and maintain to the satisfaction of the licensing authority adequate staff and adequate laboratory facilities for carrying out tests of strength, quality and purity of the substances manufactured by him or

   (ii) make arrangements with some institution approved by the licensing authority for such tests to be regularly carried out on his behalf by the institution.

(5) The licensee shall maintain reference samples

from each batch of the drugs manufactured by him in a quantity which is atleast twice the quantity of the drug required to conduct all the tests performed on the batch. In case of drugs bearing an expiry date on the label the reference samples shall be maintained for a period of three months beyond the date of expiry of potency. In case of drug where no date of expiry or potency is specified on the label the reference sample shall be maintained for a period of 3 years from the date of manufacture.

(6) The licensee shall maintain an inspection book to enable an inspector to record his impressions and the defects noticed.

The licensee who has been granted a licence shall for Schedule C and CI and X drugs :

(i) forward to the licensing authority of the concerned States of manufacture and supply of the drug a statement of the sales effected to the manufacturers, wholesalers, retailers, hospitals, dispensaries and nursing homes and Registered Medical Practitioners every three months;

(ii) maintain accounts of all transactions giving details as indicated below in a register bound and serially page numbered and such records shall be retained for a period of five years or one year after the expiry of potency, whichever is later.

A. Accounts of the drugs specified in Schedule X used for the manufacture:

1. Date of issue.
2. Name of the drug.
3. Opening balance of stock on the production day.
4. Quantity received, if any, and source from where received.

5. Quantity used in manufacture.
6. Balance quantity on hand at the end of the production day.
7. Signature of the person incharge.

B. Accounts of production:

1. Date of manufacture.
2. Name of the drug.
3. Batch Number.
4. Quantity of raw material used in manufacture.
5. Anticipated yield.
6. Actual yield.
7. Wastage.
8. Quantity of the manufactured goods transferred.

C. Accounts of the manufactured drugs:

1. Date of manufacture.
2. Name of the drug.
3. Batch Number.
4. Opening Balance.
5. Quantity manufactured.
6. Quantity sold.
7. Name of the purchaser and his address.
8. Balance quantity at the end of the day.

D. The licensee shall store drugs specified in Schedule X in bulk form and when any of such drug is required for manufacture in a place other than its place of storage it shall be kept in a separate place under the direct custody of a responsible person.

E. The licensee shall comply, with the requirements of 'God Manufacturing Practices' as laid down in Schedule M.

Further application after rejection can be applied within 6 months and after the inspection of the Central licence approving authority is satisfied the licence is granted to them.

Any person who is aggrieved by the order passed by the licensing authority may within thirty days from the date of receipt of such order appeal to the State Government or the Central Government may after such enquiry into the matter as is considered necessary and give him opportunity for representing his views.

Prohibition for the manufacture for sale of cyclamates and preparation containing cyclamates.

If any one is not complying with the rules as laid down by Central licence authority then these licences can be either cancelled or suspended before its expiry.

MANUFACTURE FOR EXAMINATION, TEST OR ANALYSIS

If the person proposes to manufacture a drug for the purpose of examination, test or analysis he is required to obtain a licence.

The licence is valid for a period of one year unless sooner cancelled.

CONDITIONS OF LICENCE

(1) The licensee shall use the drugs manufactured under the licence exclusively for purpose of examination, test or analysis and shall carry on the manufacture and examination, test or analysis at the place specified in the licence.

(2) The licensee shall allow any inspector to enter with or without notice, the premises where the drugs are manufactured and to satisfy himself that only examination test or analysis work is being conducted.

(3) The licensee shall keep a record of the quantity of drugs manufactured for the examination, test or analysis and of any person or persons to whom the drugs have been supplied.

(4) The licensee shall comply with such further requirements if applicable to the holders of the licences as may be specified in any sales subsequently made under the Act and of which the licensing authority has given him not less than one month's notice.

(5) The licensee shall maintain an inspection book to enable an inspector to record his impressions and defects noticed.

If the licensee has failed to comply with any of the conditions of the licence, then his licence will be cancelled and a licensee whose licence has been suspended or cancelled may appeal to the State Government within three months of the date of the order.

LABELLING AND PACKING OF DRUGS

The following particulars shall be either printed or written in indelible ink and shall appear in a conspicuous manner on the label of innermost container of any drug and on any drug and on every other coverings in which the container is packed namely—

(i) The name of the drug:

(A) For this purpose], [the proper name of the drug shall be printed or written in a more conspicuous manner than the trade name, if any which shall be shown immediately after or under the proper name and shall be]—

(a) for drugs included in Schedule F or Schedule F(I), the name given therein

(b) for drugs included in the Indian Pharmacopoeia or the official pharmacopoeias and official compendia of drug standards prescribed in Rule 124, the name or synonym specified in the respective official pharmacopoeias and official compendia of drug standards followed by the letters 'I.P.' or, as the case may be, by the recognised abbreviations of the respective official pharmacopoeia and official compendia of drug standards;

(c) for drugs included in the National Formulary of India, the name or synonym specified therein followed by the letters 'N.F.I.';

(d) for other drugs, the international non-proprietary name, if any, published by the World Health Organisation or where an international non-proprietary name is not published, the name descriptive of the true nature or origin of the substance.

(B) The following preparations shall be labelled only with proper name of the drug and not with any trade name:

(a) Preparations containing any new drug as the single active ingredient and approved under Rule 30-A, 69-B or 75-B by the licensing authority subject to the condition that such preparations should be marketed under a generic name only.

(b) Preparations containing any drug specified in Schedule W as the single active ingredient.]

(ii) A correct statement of the net content in terms of weight, measure, volume, number of units of contents, number of units of activity, as the case may be, and the weight, measure and volume shall be expressed in Metric system.

(iii) The content of active ingredients:

This shall be expressed—

(a) for oral liquid preparations in terms of the content per single dose, the dose being indicated in 5 millilitres or multiple thereof:

Provided that where the dose is below 5 millilitres the contents of active ingredients may be expressed in terms of one millilitre [or fraction thereof]:

(b) for liquid parenteral preparations ready for administration, in terms of 1 millilitre of percentage by volume or per dose in the case of a single dose container:

Provided that if the preparation is contained in an ampoule it will be enough if the composition is shown on the lable or wrapper affixed to any package in which such ampoule is issued for sale;

(c) for drugs in solid form intended for parenteral administration in terms of units or weight per milligramme or gramme;

(d) for tablets, capsules, pills and the like, in terms of the content in each tablet, capsule, pill or other unit, as the case may be;

(e) for other preparations, in terms of percentage by weight or volume or in terms of unitage per gram or millilitre as the case may be:

Provided that clause (iii) shall not apply to a pharmacopoeial preparation where the composition of such preparation is specified in the respective pharmacopoeia and to a preparation included in the National Formulary of India;

(iv) [The name of the manufacturer and the address of the premises of the manufacturer where the drug has been manufactured.]

Provided that if the drug is contained in an ampoule or a similar small container, it shall be enough if only the name of the manufacturer and his principal place of manufacture is shown.

(v) A distinctive batch number, that is to say, the number by reference to which details of manufacture of the particular batch from which the substance in the container is taken are recorded and are available for inspection, the figure representing the batch number being preceded by the words 'Batch No.' or 'B. No.' or 'Batch' or 'Lot No.' 'Lot'.

(vi) Every drug manufactured in India shall bear on its label the number of the licence under which the drug is manufactured, the figure representing the manufacturing licence number being preceded by the words 'Manufacturing Licence Number' or 'Mfg. Lic. No.' or 'M.L.'.

(vii) Drugs specified in Schedule P and their preparations including combinations with other drugs shall bear on their labels the date of manufacture and the date of expiry of potency, and the period between the date of manufacture and the date of expiry shall not exceed that laid down in the said Schedule [under the conditions of storages specified therein. Drugs preparations not included in Schedule P, shall bear on their labels the date of their manufacture and also the date of their expiry which shall not exceed sixty months from the date of manufacture]: Provided that this period may be extended by the licensing authority specified in clause (b) of Rule 21 in respect of any specified drug if satisfactory evidence is produced by the manufacturer to justify such an extension.

(viii) Drugs specified in Schedule C(I) and their preparations including combinations with other drugs shall bear on the labels (a) the date of manufacture, (b) date of expiry of potency fixed by the manufacturer, and (c) where such drugs are imported, also the number of licence under which the drug is imported, preceded by the words 'Import Licence':

Provided that drugs in bulk form included in Schedule C(I) which are not ready for use and not included in Schedule P need not bear on the label the date of expiry of potency.]

Provided further that no reference shall be made to any other licence number granted by any authority outside India on any label or container or in any covering in which the container is packed or in any other matter or advertisement enclosed therewith.

(ix) Every drug intended for distribution to the medical profession as a free sample shall, while complying with the labelling provisions under clauses (i) to (viii), further bear on the label of the container the words 'Physicians' sample—Not to be sold' which shall be overprinted.

(x) If any preparation contains not less than 3 per cent by volume of alcohol the quantity of alcohol shall be stated in terms of the average percentage by volume of absolute alcohol in the finished products.

(xi) in addition to the other particulars which are required to be printed or written under these rules, the label of innermost container of the following categories of drugs and every other covering in which the container is packed shall bear a conspicuous red vertical line on the left side running throughout the body of the label which should not be less than 1 mm in width and without disturbing the other conditions printed on the label under these rules, namely—

Narcotic analgesics, hypnotics, sedatives, tranquillisers, corticosteroids, hormones, hypoglycemics, antimicrobials, antiepileptics, antidepressants, anticoagulants, anti-cancer drugs and all other drugs falling under Schedules 'G', 'H', and 'X' whether covered or not in the above list:

Provided that the provisions of this clause shall not apply to,—

(a) preparations intended for animal treatment;

(b) preparations intended for external use;

(c) Ophthalmic preparations and ear drops; and

(d) Sterile preparations such as sutures, surgical dressings and preparations intended for parenteral use.}

(2) (i) The particulars to be printed or written on the label of a mechanial contraceptive shall be as specified in Schedule R.

(ii) The following particulars, in addition to those specified under sub-rule (1) shall be either printed or written in indelible ink and shall appear in a conspicuous manner on the label of the innermost container and on every other covering in which the container of a contraceptive, other than a mechanical contraceptive, is packed, namely :

(a) the date of manufacture;

(b) the date up to which the contraceptive is expected to retain its properties;

(c) the storage conditions necessary for preserving the properties of the contraceptive up to the date indicated in sub-clause (b):

Provided that for oral contraceptives it shall be sufficient to display on the label of the container the date of manufacture only.

(3) (i) The particulars prescribed in sub-rule (1) shall be printed or written in indelible ink either on the label borne by a container or vaccine lymph or on a label or wrapper affixed to any package in which the container is issued for sale. The said particulars shall be indelibly marked on the sealed container of surgical ligature or suture or printed or written in indelible ink on a label enclosed therein.

(ii) Nothing in these rules shall be deemed to require the labelling of any transparent cover or of any wrapper, case or other covering used solely for the purpose of packing, transport or delivery.

(4) Where by any provision of these rules any particulars are required to be displayed on a label on the container. Such particulars may, instead of being displayed on a label, be etched, painted or otherwise indelibly marked on the container:

Provided that, except where otherwise provided in these

rules, the name of the drug or any distinctive letters intended to refer to the drug shall not be etched, painted or otherwise indelibly marked on any glass container other than ampoules.

Explanation.—For the purpose of this rule, the date of expiry shall be in terms of month and year and it shall mean that the drug is recommended till the last day of the month. The date of expiry shall be preceded by the words 'Expiry date'.]

Labelling of medicines.—(1) The container of a medicine for internal use shall—

(a) if it contains a substance specified in Schedule G, be labelled with the words 'Caution: it is dangerous to take this preparation except under medical supervision'—conspicuously printed and surrounded by a line within which there shall be no other words;

(b) if it contains a substance specified in Schedule H be labelled with the symbol Rx and conspicuously displayed on the left top corner of the label and be also labelled with the following words:

'Schedule H drug—Warning: To be sold by retail on the prescription of a Registered Medical Practitioner only.';

(c) if it contains a substance specified in Schedule H and comes within the purview of the Dangerous Drugs Act, 1930 be labelled with the symbol NRx which shall be in red and conspicuously displayed on the left top corner of the label, and be also labelled with the following words:

'Schedule H drug—Warning: To be sold by retail on the prescription of a Registered Medical Practitioner only.';

(d) if it contains a substance specified in Schedule X, be labelled with the symbol XRx which shall be in red conspicuously displayed on the left top corner of the label, and be also labelled with the following words:

'Schedule X drug–Warning: To be sold by retailer on the prescription of a Registered Medical Practitioner only.'

(2) The container of an embrocation, liniment, lotion, liquid antiseptic or other liquid medicine for external application shall be labelled with the words in capital 'For External use only'.

(3) The container of a medicine made up ready only for treatment of an animal shall be labelled conspicuously with the words 'Not for human use; for animal treatment only' and shall bear a symbol depicting the head of a domestic animal.

(4) The container of a medicine prepared for treatment of human ailments shall if the medicine contains industrial methylated spirit, indicate this fact on the label and be labelled with the words:

"For External use only".

(5) Substances specified in Schedule X in bulk form shall bear a label wherein the symbol as specified in sub-rule (1) shall be given conspicuously in red letters.

Non-Sterile Surgical Ligature and Suture.—Every container of, and wrapper enclosing surgical ligature or suture other than a ligature or suture offered or intended to be offered for sale as sterile, shall bear a label on which are printed or written in a conspicuous manner in indelible red ink the words "Non-sterile surgical ligature (suture)—not to be used for operations upon the human body unless efficiently sterilized".

(2) The name and address of the manufacturer shall be printed on the label of the container of a patent or proprietary medicine.

(3) The true formula or list of the ingredients shall be printed or written in indelible ink on the outer label of every package containing patent or proprietary medicine.

Use of letters I.P. etc.—The letters 'I.P.' and recognised abbreviations of pharmacopoeias and official compendia of drug standards prescribed under these rules shall be entered on the label of the drug only for the purpose of indicating that the drug is in accordance with standards set out in the Indian Pharmacopoeia or in any such pharmacopoeia or official compendium of drug standards recognised under the Rule.]

Prohibition against altering inscriptions on containers, labels or wrappers of drug.—No person shall alter, obliterate or deface any inscription or mark made or recorded by the manufacturer on the container label or wrapper of any drug:

Provided that nothing in this rule shall apply to any alteration, any inscription or mark made on the container, label or wrapper of any drug at the instance or direction or with the permission of the licensing authority.

Packing of drugs.—(1) The pack sizes of drugs meant for retail sale shall be as prescribed in Schedule P-1 to these rules.

(2) The pack sizes of drugs not covered by the Schedule P-1 shall be as given below:

Unless specified otherwise in Schedule P-1,

(i) The pack sizes for Tablets/Capsules shall be—

Where the number of Tablets (coated or uncoated)/Capsules (hard or soft geletine) is less than 10, such packing shall be made by the integral number. For numbers above 10, the pack sizes of Tablets/Capsules shall contain multiple of 5.

(ii) The pack sizes for liquid Oral preparations shall be 30 ml. (paediatric only) 60 ml./100 ml./200 ml./450 ml.

(iii) The pack sizes for Paediatric Oral Drops shall be 5 ml./10 ml./15 ml.

(iv) The pack sizes for Eye/Ear/Nasal drops shall be 3 ml./5 ml./10 ml.

(v) The pack sizes for Eye Ointment shall be 3 gm./ 5 gm./ 10 gm.

Provided that the provisions of the pack sizes covered under this rule shall not apply to:

1. Pack sizes or dosages forms not covered by the foregoing provisions of this rule.
2. The imported formulations in finished form.
3. Preparations intended for Veterinary use.
4. Preparations intended for Export.
5. Vitamins/Tonics/Cough Preparations/Antacids/ Laxatives in Liquid Oral forms, Unit dose (including applicaps).
6. Pack sizes of dosage forms meant for retail sale to Hospitals, Registered Medical Practitioners, Nursing Homes.
7. Physician' Samples.
8. Pack sizes of Large Volume intravenous Fluids.

Provided also that pack sizes of any of the new drug as and when approved by the Licensing Authority appointed under Rule 21 and if not covered under this rule, shall be examined for the purpose of approval with specific justification by the said Licensing Authority.

Packing of drugs specified in Schedule X.—The drugs sepcified in Schedule X shall be marketed in packings not exceeding—

(i) 100 unit doses in the case of tablets/capsules;

(ii) 300 ml. in the case of oral liquid preparation;

(iii) and 5 ml. in the case of injections;

Provided that nothing in this rule shall apply to packing meant for use of a hospital or a dispensary subject to the conditions that—

(i) such supplies are made by the manufacturers or distributors direct to the hospitals/dispensaries; and

(ii) hospital packs shall not be supplied to a retail dealer or to a Registered Medical Practitioner.

Diseases which a drug may not purport to prevent or cure.—(1) No drug may purport or claim to prevent or cure or may convey to the intending user thereof any idea that it may prevent or cure, one or more of the diseases of ailments specified in Schedule J.

(2) No drug may purport or claim to procure or assist to procure, or may convey to the intending user thereof any idea that it may procure or assist to procure, miscarriage in women.

Exemption of certain drugs from certain provisions of this part

(1) Labels on packages or containers of the drugs for export shall be adapted to meet the specific requirements of the law of country to which the drug is to be exported but the following particulars shall appear in conspicuous position as

— Name of the drug.

— Name, address of the manufacturer and the number of licence under which the drug has been manufactured.

— batch or lot number.

— date of expiry (if any).

If the drug is classified under Schedule F, Schedule F(I) an Schedule X, blood products, Narcotic and Psychotropic Substances are not labelled with the name and address of the manufacturer, the labels on packages or containers bear a code number as approved by the licensing authority.

(2) The labelling requirements shall not apply to a medicine made up ready for treatment whether after or without dilution which is supplied on the prescription of a registered medical practitioner provided that the medicine is labelled with the following particulars.

(a) The name and address of the supplier.

(b) The name of the patient and the quantity of

the medicine.

(c) The number representing serial number of the entry in the prescription register.

(d) The dose, if the medicine is for internal use.

(e) The words 'For External use only' shall be printed on the label if the medicine is for external application.

SPECIAL PROVISIONS RELATING TO BIOLOGICAL AND OTHER SPECIAL PRODUCTS

(1) Name of Substance: If any of the Schedule C and C(I) product is advertised or sold the proper name as stated in Schedule F(I) shall appear on the label.

(2) Container

(i) No substance specified in Schedule C shall be sold or offered for sale unless it has been sealed in a previously sterilised container made of glass or any other suitable material approved by licensing authority or it shall not be necessary to use a previously sterilised container if the filled and sealed container is to be sterilised after the sealing and such sterilising procedure would render the products sterile.

(ii) When any such substance is in liquid form and portion of substance can be withdrawn for use, the liquid should contain a sufficient proportion of some antiseptic to prevent growth of any organism.

(iii) The container shall comply with requirements as specified in Schedule F or Schedule F(I).

(3) Labelling

(1) The particulars as specified in Schedule F or Schedule F(I) shall be written on every container—

(i) Where a drug is imported the number of licence under which it is imported, preceded by the words 'Import Licence'.

(ii) Where a test for potency in units is required a statement of the potency in units defined in terms of related standard preparation but this shall not apply in the case of vaccine lymph.

(iii) Where a test for potency of maximum toxicity is required the date of expiry shall be preceded by the words 'Expiry date' and this should be in terms of month and year, means the drug is recommended for use till the last day of month.

(2) The particulars should be written in indelible ink on the container and enclosed even in the sealed container of surgical ligature or suture.

(3) The particulars as specified in Schedule F that is

(i) date of manufacture or completion of final product.

(ii) Nature and proportion of antiseptic.

(iii) The precaution necessary for preserving the properties of contents.

(4) For the purpose of Act the date of manufacture of a batch is completed shall be

— in cases where a test for potency or toxicity is required, the date on which the substance was removed from cold storage after having been kept at a temperature not exceeding 5°C continuously for a period not exceeding two years from the time when the last test was completed.

— where no such test is required

(i) if the substance is a serum obtained from a living animal, the earliest date on which any material contributing to the batch was removed from the animal.

(ii) if the substance was obtained by the growth of organisms on artificial media the earliest date on which growth was terminated in any of the material contributing to the batch.

— in other cases, the date on which the substance is filled in the container.

STANDARDS—Every substance supecified in Schedule C and C(I) should comply with the standards of strength, quality and purity as specified in Schedule F and F(I).

Test for Strength and Quality : The tests specified are—

(i) Tests for sterility

(ii) Test for freedom from abnormal toxicity

(iii) Test for pyrogens

(iv) Test for determining strength, quality and purity of substance.

The substance should be stored in a cool place and away from light.

STANDARDS

Standards of drugs.—(1) Drugs included in the Indian Pharmacopoeia:

(i) The standards for identity, purity and strength shall be those as may be specified in the edition of the Indian Pharmacopoeia for the time being in force.

(ii) In case the standards for identity, purity and strength for drugs are not specified in the edition of the Indian Pharmacopoeia for the time being in force but are specified in the edition of the Indian Pharmacopoeia immediately preceding, the standards for identity, purity and strength shall be those occurring in such immediately preceding edition of the Indian Pharmacopoeia.

(2) For other drugs :

(i) The standards for identity, purity and strength shall be those as may be specified in the edition of the official pharmacopoeia, for the time being in force, of any country to which the drug claims to comply with.

(ii) In case the standards for identity, purity and strength for drugs are not specified in the edition of such official pharmacopoeia, for the time being in force, but are specified in the edition immediately preceding, the standards for identity, purity and strength shall be those occurring in such immediately preceding edition of such official pharmacopoeia to which the drug claims to comply with.

(iii) For drugs for which standards are not included in the edition of the official pharmacopoeia, for the time being in force, of any country or in its edition immediately preceding, but included in the official compendia of drugs standards, namely, the British Pharmaceutical Codex or the National Formulary of the United States, for the time being in force, to which the drug claims to comply with.

Standards for veterinary drugs.—For drugs intended for veterinary use, the standards shall be those given in the current edition for the time being in force of the British Veterinary Codex.

Standards for patent or proprietary medicines.—The standards for patent or proprietary medicines shall be those laid down in Schedule V and such medicines shall also comply with the standards laid down in the Second Schedule to the Act.

Standards for Surgical Dressings.—The standards for surgical dressings shall be such as are laid down in Schedule F(II).

Standards for Sterilised Umbilical tapes.—The Standards for Sterilised Umbilical tapes shall be as laid down in Schedule F(III).

Standards for substance (other than food) intended to affect the structure or any function of human body—contraceptives.—(1) The standards for mechanical contraceptives shall be such as are laid down in Schedule R.

(2) The standards which other contraceptives will have to comply with shall be in conformity with the formulae approved as safe and efficacious by the Central Government. Such formula shall be displayed on the label of every container of such contraceptive.

Standards for Medical Devices.—The standards for the medical devices shall be such as are laid down in Schedule R-I

Standards for Disinfectants

The standards for disinfectants shall be such as are laid down in Schedule O.

Standards for ophthalmic preparations.—The standards for ophthalmic preparations shall be those laid down in Schedule FF, and such preparations shall also comply with the standards set out in the Second Schedule to the Act.

List of colours permitted to be used in drugs.—(1) No drug shall contain a colour other than that specific below :

(1) *Natural Colours*

Annatto

Carotene

Chlorophyll

Cochineal

Curcumin

Red Oxide of iron

Yellow Oxide of iron

[Titanium Oxide]

[Black Oxide of iron]

(2) *Artificial Colours*

Caramel

[Riboflavin]

(3) *Coal Tar Colours*

Common name of the colour	*Colour Index Number*	*Chemical Name*
1	2	3
GREEN		
Quinazarine Green S.S.	61565	1,4-bis (p-Toluino)-anthraquinone.
Alizrin Cyanine Green F.	61570	Di-sodium salt of 1, 4-bis (O-Sulfo-p-toluino) anthraquinone.
[Fast Green FCF.	42053	Di-sodium salt of 4-{[4-(N-ethyl-p-sulfo-benzylamino)-phenyl-}-4-hydroxy-2-sulfoniumphenyl-methylene} [1-N-ethyl-N-p-sulfobenzyl-1-Δ 2, 5,-cyclohexadienimine]
Green S.	44090	Monosodium salt of 4, 4 bis (dimethyl-animo)-diphenylmethylene-(2-naphthol-3, 6-disulphonic acid).]
YELLOW		
Tartrazine	19140	Tri-sodium salt of 3-carboxy-5-hydroxy-1-p-sulfophenyl-4-p-sulfophenyl-azopyrazole.
Sunset Yellow FCF.	15985	Di-sodium salt of 1-p-sulfophenyl-azo-2-naphthol-6-sulfonic acid.
[Quinoiine Yellow WS.	47005	Di-sodium salt of di-sulfonic acid of 12-(2-quinolyl)-1, 3-indandione.
RED		
Amarnath	16185	Tri-sodium salt of 1-(4-sulfo-1-napthy-lazo) 2-naphthol 3, 6-di-sulfonic acid.

Sale of Drugs

The state government shall appoint licensing authorities to issue licences for the following categories :

(1) A licence to sell, stock or exhibit or distribute drugs other then those specified in Schedule C, C(1) and X and by retail on restricted licence or by wholesale shall be issued in Form 20, 20-A, 20B.

(2) A licence to sell, stock or exhibit or distribute drugs specified in Schedules and (1) excluding

those specified in Schedule by retail on restricted licence or by wholesale shall be issued in Form 21, Form 21A or 21B.

(3) A licence to sell, stock or exhibit for sale or distribute drugs specified in Schedule X by retail or by wholesale shall be issued in the Form 20F or 20G.

The licences to vend drugs are issued only with respect to drugs other than those specified in Schedule C and C(1) Travelling agents of firms, may however are permit to distribute samples of Schedule C&C, drugs to the medical professional, hospitals, dispensaries, medical institutions or research institutions.

In granting a licence the authority empowered to grant it shall have regard to the number of licences granted in the locality during one year immediately preceding and the occupation, trade or business carried on by such applicant. Any person who is aggrieved by the order passed by the licensing authority can appeal within 30 days.

The premises should be specified as–

(1) **Drugs Store**–It should be displayed at such establishments who do not require the services of a qualified person.

(2) **Chemists and Druggist**–Shall be displayed by such licensees who employ the services of a 'Qualified person' but who do not maintain a 'Pharmacy' for compounding against prescription.

(3) **'Pharmacy'** 'Pharmacist' Dispensing chemists or Pharmaceutical Chemists shall be displayed by such licensees who employ the services of a 'Qualified person' and maintain a 'Pharmacy' for compounding against prescription.

"Qualified Person" means a person who–

(a) holds a diploma or degree in pharmacy or parmaceutical chemistry of an institute approved by the licensing authority or

(b) is a registered pharmacist as defined in the Pharmacy Act 1948.

(c) has not less than four years practical experience of dispensing which is in the opinion of the licensing authority

Wholesale of Drugs

Licences are necessary for wholesale for the following classes of drugs:

(1) Schedules C and C(1) drugs & Sch X

(2) All other drugs not specified in Sch. C and C(1)

Conditions for the grant of licence for wholesale of Sch. C and C(1) drugs. & Sch X

(1) The licencee must have premises not less than 10 square meters equipped with facilities for proper storage of drugs with a view to preserve the pitency..

(2) The drugs should be sold only to those person who are licensed to retail them.

(3) The licensee shall maintain an Inspection Book to enable an inspector to record his impression and the defects noticed.

(4) No drugs shall be sold or stocked by the licensee after the date of expiration of potency recorded on its container.

(5) Records should be maintained of all purchases and sales of Sch. C&C, & Sch X drugs as for

Sch C&C(1)–

(i) Dates of purchases and sales

(ii) Name and address of the firms from whom purchased and of the firms to whom sold.

(iii) Names and quantities of the drugs and their Batch number.

(iv) Names of the manufacturer of the drug.

The records are required to be preserved for a period of atleast three years from the date of sale.

Schedule 'X'

(i) Date of transection

(ii) Quantity received, if any the name and address of the supplier and the number of the relevant licence held by the supplier.

(iii) Name of the drug

(iv) Quantity supplied

(v) Manufacturers name

(vi) Batch No. or Lot No.

(vii) Name and address of the patient/purchasers

(viii) Reference Number of the prescription against which supplies were made.

(ix) Bill no and date in respect of purchases and supplies made by him.

(x) Signature of person under whose supervision the drugs have been supplied.

(6) Licence should be displayed in a prominent part of the premises open to public

Conditions for the grant of licences for wholesale of drugs other than those specified in Sch. C & C,

(1) The drugs should not be sold to any person who does not hold a licence for the retail sale or distribution of drugs, however this condition does not apply for the distribution to hospitals dispensaries, samples to registered medical practioners or officers authorised by Government for the purchase of drug.

(2) The licence should be displayed on a prominent position in the part of premises open to public

(3) All other provisions of the Act and the Rules as discussed above should be observed as for as applicable.

Retail Sale of Drugs: Licences are necessary for retail sale of drugs. There are two categories of licences issued :

(i) **General Licences** : These are granted to those persons who engage the services of qualified persons and their establishments are either 'Pharmacy' or 'Chemists & Druggists'

(ii) **Restricted Licences**--These licences are granted to persons who do not engage the services of qualified persons and their establishments are drug stores and who deals in such classes of drugs whose sale can be effected without qualified supervision.

Conditions for grant of **General Licences**--

(1) The licensee must have adequate premises equipped with facilities for proper storage under the charge of a qualified person.

(2) If a person licensed to sell Schedule C and C1 drugs wishes to sell any additional categories of such drugs as are not listed in his licence, he must obtain the permission of the licensing authority to do.

(3) Requirement prescribed for a pharmacy in Schedule N must be fulfilled.

(4) All the records should be maintained as per the provision of the act and preserved atleast for a period of two years from the date of last entry.

(5) Licensee must kept an inspection book and allow the inspector to inspect the premises.

(6) Licensee must report within a month any change in the qualified staff.

(7) No Schedule C and C(1) drugs should be sold or exhibited for sale until due precautions, have been taken for their storage.

Conditions for the grant of **Restricted Licenses.**

(1) The licensee can deal only in those drugs which can be sold without the supervision of qualified person.

(2) Drugs should be sold in their original containers.

(3) The licence should be prominently displayed in

the premises.

(4) Licensee must take adequate precautions for preserving the properties of the drugs.

Supply of Drugs Against General Licence

(1) Any drug if compounded or made on the licence's premises be compounded or made it should be under the direct supervision of qualified person.

(2) (i) The supply of any drugs other than those specified in Schedule X on a prescription of a registered medical practioners shall be recorded at the time of supply in the prescription register. The option to maintain a prescription register or cash or credit memo book in respect of drugs and medicines which are supplied from or in the original container shall be made in writing to the licensing authority at the time of application for the grant or renewal of licence. The following particulars shall be entered–

(a) Serial number of entry

(b) the date of supply

(c) the name and address of prescriber

(d) the name and address of the patient

(e) the name of the drug or preparation and the quantity

(f) in the case of drug specified in Sch C or Sch. H the name of manufacturer of drug, its batch number and the date of expiry of potency, if any

(g) the signature of the qualified person by or under whose supervision the medicine was made up or supplied.

(ii) It shall not be necessary to record the above details in register if any drugs supplied under the Employees State Insurance Scheme

(iii) Any drug other than that specified in Sch. C or Sch. H if it is supplied in original unopened container of the manufacturer and if the prescription is duly stamped with the name of supplier.

(iv) In case of Sch. C drugs the above mentioned particulars are required to be entered in the register.

(3) (i) The supply of any drug should be made, against cash/credit memo which shall contain:

(a) Name, address and sale licence number of dealer

(b) Serial number of the cash/credit memo

(c) the name and quantity of the drug supplied.

(ii) Carbon copies of cash/credit memoes shall be maintained by the licensee as record.

(4) Records of purchase of a drug intended for sale by relail shall be maintained by the licensee and such records shall show the following particulars :

(i) the date of purchase;

(ii) the name and address of the person from whom purchased and number of the relevant licence held by him;

(iii) the name of the drug, the quantity and the batch number;

(iv) the name of the manufacturer of the drug;

(v) purchase bills including cash or credit memos shall be serially numbered by licensee;

(5) (i) Substances specified in Sch. H or Sch. X shall not be sold by retail except on and in accordance with the prescription of a Registered Medical Practioners and in case of

substance specified in Sch. X, the prescription shall be in duplicate, one copy of which shall be retained by the licensee for a period of two years.

(ii) The supply of drugs specified in Sch. H or Sch. X to registered Medical Practioners Hospitals, Dispensaries and Nursing Homes shall be made only against the signed order in writing which shall be preserved by the licensee for a period of two years.

(6) The person dispensing a prescription containing a drug specified in Sch. H and Sch. X shall comply with the following requirements in addition to other requirements :

(i) the prescription must not be dispensed more than once unless the prescriber has stated thereon that it may be dispensed more than once in accordance with the stated intervals and directions.

(ii) At the time of dispensing, there must be noted on the prescription on above the signature of the prescriber the name and address of the seller and the date on which the prescription is dispensed.

(7) No person dispensing a prescription containing substances specified in Sch. H or X may supply any other preparations whether containing the save substances or not in lieu thereof.

(8) Substances specified in Sch. X kept in retail stores should be either stored under lock and key in Cupboard reserved solely for the storage of these substances or in a part of the premises separated from the remainder of the premises.

(9) No drug shall be sold or stocked by the licensee after the date of expiration of period recorded on its container, label or wrapper.

(10) The supply by retail of any drug in an container

other than the one in which the manufacturer has marketed the drug, shall be made only dealers who employ qualified persons and such supply shall be made in an envelope with following particulars–

(i) name of the drug

(ii) quantity supplied

(iii) the name and address of the dealer

(11) The supply of drugs specified in Sch. X shall be recorded at the time of supply in a register (bound and serially page numbered) specially maintained for the purpose and separate pages shall be allotted for each drug. The following particulars shall be entered in the register–

(i) Date of transaction

(ii) Quantity received, if any, the name and address of the supplier and the number of the relevant licence held by supplier.

(iii) Name of drug

(iv) Quality supplied.

(v) Manufacturer's name.

(vi) Batch number or lot number.

(vii) Name and address of the patient/purchaser.

(viii) Reference number of the prescription against which supplies were made.

(ix) Bill number and date in respect of purchases and supplies made by him.

(x) Signature of the person under whose supervision the drugs have been supplied.

Additional information to be furnished by an applicant for licence to the licensing authority : The applicant for the grant of a licence should provide documentory evidence in respect of the ownership or occupation on rental or other basis of the premises, specified in the application for licence or in the licence granted, constitution of the firm, or any other relevant matter which may be required for the purpose of verifying correctness of the statements made by the applicant or the licensee while applying for or after obtaining the licence as the case may be.

Cancellation and Suspension of Licences– The licensing authority may after giving the licensee an opportunity to show cause to cancel a licence issued or suspend it for such period as he thinks fit either wholly or in respect of some of the substances to which it relates, if in his opinion the licensee has failed to comply with any of the conditions of the licence or with any provisions of the act or rules there under.

Provided that, where such failure or contravention is the consequence of an act or ommission on the part of an agent or employee, the licence shall not be cancelled or suspended if the licensee proves to the satisfaction of licensing authority.

(i) that the act or ommission was not instigated or conrived at by him on if the licensee is a firm or company, by a partner of the firm or director of the company or

(ii) that he or his agent or employee had not been guilty of any similar act or omission within tweleve months before the date on which the act or omission in question took place, or where his agent or employee had been guilty of any such act or omission, the licensee had not or could not reasonably have had knowledge of that previous act or omission or

(iii) if the act or omission was a continuing act or omission, he had not or could not reasonably have had knowledge of that previous act or omission or

(iv) that he had used due diligence to insure that the conditions of the licence or the provision of the Act or the rules thereunder were observed.

A licensee whose licence has been suspended or cancelled may within three months of the date of order, prefer an appeal against that order to the State Government which shall decide the same.

Procedure for Disposal of Drugs in the event of Cancellation of Licence

(1) In case of a licensee, whose licence has been cancelled desires to dispose of the drugs he has been in possession in his premises in respect of which the licence has been cancelled, he shall apply in writing to the licensing authority for this purpose, giving the following particulars namely–

(i) the name and address of the person to whom the drugs are proposed to be sold or supplied together with the number of the licence for sale or manufacture, as the case may be held by him.

(ii) The names of drugs together with their quantities, batch number, the names and addresses of their, if any proposed to be sold to the person mentioned in clause (a).

(2) The licensing authority may after examination of the particulars and if necessary after inspection by an inspector of the premises where the drugs are stocked, grant the necessary permission for their disposal.

Application for loan licence to manufacture cosmetics.– (1) Application for grant or renewal of a loan licence for the manufacture for sale of cosmetics shall be made in Form 31-A to the licensing authority and shall be accompanied by a fee of rupees two hundred.

Explanation– For the purpose of this rule a 'loan licence' means a licence which a licensing authority may issue to an applicant who does not have his own arrangements for manufacture but who intends to avail himself of the manufacturing facilities owned by a licensee in Form 32.

(2) If a person applies for the renewal of a loan licence

after its expiry but within six months of such expiry, the fee payable for the renewal of such a licence shall be [93](rupees two hundred) plus an additional fee at the rate of [93](rupees seventy-five) per month or part thereof.

(3) The licensing authority shall, before the grant of a loan licence, satisfy himself that the manufacturing unit has adequate equipment, staff, capacity for manufacture and facilities to undertake the manufacture on behalf of the applicant for loan licence.

(4) The loan licence shall be granted by the licensing authority to only such applicants who propose to avail of the facilities of manufacture of cosmetics in the premises of a manufacturer located in the same state where the applicant is located. In case the manufacture of cosmetics involves any special process of manufacture or use of equipments which are not available in the state where the applicant is located, the licensing authority, after consulting the licensing authority where the manufacturing unit is located, may grant the loan licence.

(5) Subject to the provisions of sub-rule (2), application for manufacture of additional items on a loan licence shall be accompanied by a fee of rupees five for each item.

(6) A fee of [95](rupees thirty) shall be paid for a duplicate copy of a licence issued under sub-rule (1) if the original is deface, damaged or lost.)

Condition for the grant or renewal of a licence in the following conditions shall be compiled with by the applicant:

(1) The manufacture shall be conducted under the direction and personal supervision of a competent technical staff consisting of at least one person who is a whole-time employee and who possesses any one of the following qualifications–

(a) hold a Diploma in Pharmacy approved by the Pharmacy Council of India under the Pharmacy Act, 1948 (8 of 1948), or

(b) is registered under the Pharmacy Act1948 (8 of 1948), or

(c) has passed the Intermediate Examination with Chemistry as one of the subjects or an examination recognised by the Licensing Authority as equivalent to above mentioned qualifications.

(2) The factory premises shall comply with the requirements and conditions specified in Schedule M-II]

(3) The applicant shall either–

(i) provide and maintain adequate staff, premises and laboratory eqipment for testing cosmetic manufacture, and the raw materials used in the manufacture, or

(ii) make arrangements with some institution approved by the Licensing Authority [97][under Part XVI(A) of these Rules] for such tests to be regularly carried out in this behalf by the institution.

Duration of licence—An original licence or a renewed licence shall unless sooner suspended or cancelled be vabd upto the 31st December, of the year following the year in which it is granted or renewed.

[Provided that if the application for renewal of a licence in force is made before its expiry or if the application is made within six months of its expiry, after payment of additional fee, the licence shall continue to be in force until orders are passed on the application and the licence shall be deemed to have expired, if application for its renewal is not made within six months of its expiry.]

Duration of a loan licence—An original loan licence in a renewed loan licence is unless sooner suspended or cancelled, shall be valid upto the 31st December, of the year following the year in which it is granted or renewed:

Provided that if the application for the renewal of a licence is made before its expiry, or if the application is made within six months of its expiry after payment of the additional fee, the licence shall continue to be in force untill orders are passed on the application. The licence shall be deemed to have expired if the application for its renewal is not made within six months of its expiry.

Conditions of licence—A licence in Form 32 shall be subject to the conditions stated therein and to the following other conditions, namely–

(i) The licensee shall provide and maintain staff, premises and equipment as specified in Rule139.

(ii) The licensee shall comply with the provisions of the Act and the rules made thereunder and with such further requirements, if any, as may be specified in any rules to be made hereafter under Chapter IV of the Act.

(iii) The licensee shall keep records of the details of each batch of cosmetic manufactured by him and of raw materials used theiren as per particulars specified in Schedule U(1) and such records shall be retained for period of three years.]

(iv) The licensee shall test each batch or lot of the raw materials used by him for the manufacture of the cosmetics and also each batch of the final product and shall maintain records or registers showing the particulars in respect of such tests. The records or registers shall be retained for a period of three years from the date of manufacture.

(v) The licensee shall allow any [3][Inspector appointed under the Act] to enter with or without prior notice any premises where the manufacture of a substance inrespect of which the licence is issued is carried on, to inspect the premises and to take samples of the manufactured products under a receipt.

(vi) The licensee shall allow an Inspector to inspect all registers and records maintained under these rules and shall supply to the Inspector such information as they may require for the purpose of as cretaining whether the provisions of the Act and the rules made thereunder have been compiled.

(vii) The licensee shall maintain an Inspection Book

in Form 35 to enable an Inspector to record his impression and the defects noticed:

Additional information to be furnished by an applicant for licence or a licensee to the licensing authority- -The applicant for the grant of a licence or any person granted a licence under this Part shall, on demand, furnish to the licensing authority, before the grant of the licence or during the period the licence is in force, as the case may be, documentary evidence in respect of the ownership or occupation on rental or other basis of the premises, specified in the application for licence or in the licence granted, constitution of the firm, or any other relevant matter, which may be required for the purpose of verifying the correctness of the statements made by the applicant or the licensee while applying for or after obtaining the licence as the case may be.]

Conditions Loan for Manufacture of Cosmetics– (*i*) A licence in Form 32-A shall be deemed to be cancelled or suspended, if the licence owned by the licensee, in Form 32, whose manufacturing facilities, is cancelled or suspended, as the case may be under these rules.

(*ii)* The licensee shall comply with the provisions of the Act and these rules and with such further requirements, if any, as may be specified from time to time in Chapter IV of the Act, provided that where such further requirements are specified in the rules, these should come into force four months after publication in the Official Gazette.

(iii) The licensee shall keep records of the details of each batch of cosmetic manufacturerd by him and of raw materials used therein as per particulars specified in Schedule U(I) and such records shall be retained for a period of three years.]

(iv) The licensee shall test each batch or lot of the raw materials used by him for the manufacture of the cosmetics and also each batch of the final product and shall maintain records or registers showing the particulars in respect of such tests. The records or registers shall be retained for a period of three years from the date of manufacture.

(v) The licensee shall allow an Inspector appointed under the Act to enter with or without prior notice any premises where the manufacture of a substance in respect of which the licence is issued is carried on, to inspect the premises and to take samples of the manufactured products under a receipt.

(vi) The licensee shall allow an Inspector to inspect all registers and records maintained under these rules and shall supply to the Inspector such information as he may require for the purpose of ascertaining whether the provisions of the Act and the rules made thereunder have been complied.

(vii) The licensee shall maintain an Inspection Book in Form 35 to enable an Inspector to record his impressions and the defects noticed.]

Cancellation and suspension of licence

(1) The Licensing Authority may, after giving the licensee an opportunity to show cause why such an order should not be passed, by an order in writing stating the reasons therefore, cancel a licence issued under this Part or suspend it for such period as he thinks fit, either wholly or in respect of some of the substances to which it relates, if in his opinion, the license has failed to comply with any of the conditions of the licence or with any provisions of the Act or the rules made thereunder.

(2) A licensee whose licence has been suspended or cancelled may appeal within a period of three months from the date of the order to the State Government which shall after considering the appeal, pass orders, and such orders shall be final.

Prohibition of manufacture of cosmetics with Coal Tar Colour other than those prescribed–(1) No cosmetics shall be manufactured which contains a coal tar colour other than the one prescribed in Schedule Q to these rules. The coaltar colour used in the manufacture of the cosmetic shall not contain more than:

(i) 2 parts per million of arsenic calculated as arsenic trioxide.

(ii) 20 parts per million of lead calculated as lead.

(iii) 100 parts per million of heavy metals other than lead calculated as the total of the respective metals.

(2) No cosmetic intended for use on the eyebrow, or eyelash or around the eye shall be manufactured that contains any coal tar dye, coal tar dye base or coal tar dye intermediate.

Prohibition of manufacture of cosmetic containing hexachlorophene–No cosmetic containing hexachlorophene shall be manufactured.

Provided that in the case of soaps hexachlorophene may be use in concentrations not exceeding one per cent weight by weight:

Provided further that the following cautionary note shall be printed and shall appear in a conspicious manner on the wrapper of package of each soap, namely:–

"Contains hexachlorophene–not to be used on babies".

Use of Lead and Arsenic compounds for the purpose of colouring cosmetics prohibited–The use of Lead and Arsenic compounds for the purpose of colouring cosmetics is prohibited.

Form of intimation for purposes of taking samples of cosmetics.–Where an Inspector takes a sample of a cosmetic for the purpose of test or analysis, he shall intimate such purpose in writing in Form 17 to the person from whom he takes it.

Form of receipt for seized cosmetics.–A receipt by an Inspector for the stock of any cosmetics seized under clause *(c)* of sub-section (1) of Section 22 of the Act, shall be in Form 16.]

Manner of certifying copies of seized documents.— The Drugs Inspector shall return the documents, seized by him under clause *(cc)*, or produced before him under clause *(cca)*, of sub-section (1) of Section 22 of the Act, within a period of twenty days of the days of the date of such seizure or production, to the person from whom they were seized or, as the case may be the person who produced them after copies thereof or extracts therefrom have been signed by the concerned Drugs Inspector and the person from whom they were seized, or, as the case may be, who produced such records.]

Form of order not to dispose of stocks of cosmetics.—An order in writing by an Inspector under clause (*c*) of sub-section (1) of Section 22 of the Act requiring a person not to dispose of any stock of cosmetics in his possession shall be in Form 15.]

Prohibition of manufacture of cosmetic containing mercury compounds.-No cosmetic containing mercury compounds shall be manufactured.

Labelling, Packing and Standards of Cosmetics

Prohibition of sale or distribution.--Subject to the other provisions of these rules, no person shall sell or distribute any cosmetic unless the cosmetic, if of Indian origin, is manufactured by a licensed manufacturer and labelled and packed in accordance with these rules.

Exemption of Cosmetics not manufactured for consumption or sale in India from the provisions of this Part.—Labels on packages or containers of cosmetics not manufactured for comsumption or sale in India shall be adapted to meet the specific requirements, if any, of the consignee:

Provided that when a cosmetic is required by the consignee to be not labelled with the name and address of the manufacturer, the labels on packages or containers shall bear a code number as approved by the licensing authority mentioned in Rule 21.

Manner of labelling.—Subject to other provisions of the rules, a cosmetic shall carry–

(1) on both the inner and outer labels:

(i) the name of the cosmetics,

(ii) the name and the principal place of business of the manufacturer.

(2) on the outer lebel—

A declaration of the net contents expressed in terms of weight for solids, fluid measure for liquids, weight for semi-solids, combined with numerical count if the content is sub-divided:

Provided that this statement need not appear in case of a package of perfume, toilet water or like, the net content of which does not exceed 60 ml or any package of solid or semi-solid cosmetic the net content of which does not exceed 30 grams.

(3) on the inner label; where a hazard exists:

(a) Adequate direction for safe use,

(b) Any warning, caution or special direction required to be observed by the consumer,

(c) A statement of the names and quantities of the ingredients that are hazardous or poisonous.

(4) A distinctive batch number, that is to say, the number by reference to which details of manufacture of the particular batch from which the substance in the container is taken are recorded and are available for inspection the figures representing the batch number being preceded by the letter "B" Provided that this clause shall not apply to any cosmetic containing 10 grams or less if the cosmetic is in solid or semi-solid state, and 25 millilitres or less if the cosmetic is in a liquid state:]

Provided further that in the case of soap, instead of the batch number, the month and year of manufacture of soap shall be given on the label.

[14](5) Manufacturing licence number, the number being preceded by the letter 'M'.

(6) Where a package of a cosmetic has only one label such label shall contain all the information required to be shown on both the inner and the outer labels, under these rules.

Labelling of hair dyes containing coal tar colours.— Hair dyes containing para-phenylene-diamine or other coal tar dye base or coal tar dye intermediate shall be labelled with the following legend in English and local languages and these shall appear on both the inner and the outer labels:

> "*Caution.*–This product contains ingredients which may cause skin irritation in certain cases and so a preliminary test according to the accompanying directions should first be made. This product should not be used for dyeing the eyelashes or eyebrows; as such a use may cause blindness."

Each package shall also contain instructions in English and local languages on the following lines for carrying out the test:

> "This preparation may cause serious inflamation of the skin in some cases and so a preliminary test should always be carried out to determine whether or not special sensitivity exists. To make the test, cleans a small area of skin behind the ear or upon the inner surface of the forearm, using either soap and water or alcohol. Apply a small quantity of the hair dye as prepared for use to the area and allow it to dry. After twenty-four hours, wash the area gently with soap and water. If no irritation or inflammations is apparent, it may be asumed that no hypersensitivity to the dye exists. The test should, however, be carried out before each and every application. This preparation should on no account be used for dyeing eyebrows or eyelashes as severe inflammation of the eye or even blindness may result."

Special provisions relating to toothpaste containing fluoride:—

(i) Fluoride content in toothpaste shall not be more

than 1000 ppm and the content of fluoride in terms of ppm shall be mentioned on the tube and carton.

(ii) Date of expiry should be mentioned on tube and carton.

Report of result of test or analysis of cosmetics.—Test reports on samples of cosmetics taken for test or analysis under these rules shall be supplied in Form 34.

Standards for cosmetics.—Subject to the provisions of these rules, the standards for cosmetics shall be such as may be prescribed in Schedule S.

Approval of Institutions for Carrying out tests on Drugs, Cosmetics and Raw Materials used in their manufacture on behalf of Licensee for manufacture for sale of Drugs /Cosmetics

Application for grant of approval for testing drugs/ cosmetics.—(1) Application for grant or renewal of approval for carrying out tests for identity, purity, quality and strength of drugs or cosmetics or the raw materials used in the manufacture thereof on behalf of licensees for manufacture for sale of drugs or cosmetics, shall be made in Form 36 to the Licensing Authority appointed by the State Government for the purposes of Part VII, VII(A) or XIV of these rules, as the case may be and referred to as the "approving authority" under this Part and shall be accompanied by an inspection fee of rupees five hundred in the case of testing of drugs specified in Schedules C and C(1) and rupees three hundred in the case of testing of drugs other than those specified in Schedules C and C(1), homoeopathic drugs and cosmetics:

Provided that the applicant shall furnish to the approving authority such additional information as may be required by him in connection with the application in Form 36:

Provided further that if the applicant applies for renewal of approval after its expiry but within six months of such expiry, the inspection fee payable shall be rupees five hundred plus an additional inspection fee at the rate of rupees four hundred per month in the case of testing of drugs specified in Schedules C and C(1) and rupees three hundred plus an additional inspection fee of rupees two hundred per month in the case of testing of drugs other than those specified in Schedules C and C(1), homoeopathic drugs and cosmetics.

(2) A separate application shall be made for grant of approval for carrying out tests on additional categories of drugs or items of cosmetics.

Explanation.–For the purpose of this Part, the words 'drugs' and 'cosmetics' shall also mean and include the raw materials, used in the manufacture of drugs including homoeopathic drugs or cosmetics, as the case may be.

Form in which approval to be granted for carrying out tests on drugs/cosmetics on behalf of licencees for manufacture of drugs/cosmetics and conditions for grant or renewal of such approval.—(1) Approval for carryig out such tests of identity, purity, quality and strength of drugs or cosmetics as may be required under the provisions of these rules, on behalf of licensee for manufacture of drugs or cosmetics shall be granted in Form 37.

(2) Before approval in Form 37 is granted or renewed, the following conditions shall be complied with by the applicant:—

(1) The premises where the tests are being carried on shall be well lighted and properly ventilated except where the nature of tests of any drug or cosmetic warrants otherwise. Wherever necessary, the premises shall be air-conditioned so as to maintain the accuracy and functioning of laboratory instruments or to enable the performance of special tests such as sterility tests, microbiological tests, etc.

(2) The applicant shall provide adequate space having regard to the nature and number of samples of drugs of cosmetics proposed to be tested:

Provided that the approving authorities shall determine from time to time whether the space provided continues to be adequate.

(3) If it is intended to carry out tests requiring the use of animals, the applicant shall provide an animal house and comply with the following requirements:-

(i) The animal house shall be in adequate area, well lighted and properly ventilated and the animals undergoing tests shall be kept in air-conditioned area.

(ii) The animals shall be suitably housed in hygienic surroundings and necessary provision made for removal or excreta and foul smell.

(iii) The applicant shall provide for suitable arrangements for preparation of animal feed.

(iv) The applicant shall provide for suitable arrangements for quarantining of all animals immediately on their receipt in the institution.

(v) The animals shall be periodically examined for their physical fitness.

(vi) The applicant shall provide for isolation of sick animals as well as animals under test.

(vii) The applicant shall ensure compliance with the requirements of the Prevention of Cruelty to Animals Act, 1960 (59 of 1960).

(viii) The applicant shall make proper arrangements for the disposal of the carcasses of animals in a manner as not to cause hazard to public health.

(4) The applicant shall provide and maintain suitable equipment having regard to the nature and number of samples of drugs of cosmetics intended to be tested which shall be adequate in the opinion of the approving authority.

(5) The testing of drugs or cosmetics, as the case

may be, shall be under the active direction of a person whose qualifications and experience are considered adequate in the opinion of the approving authority and who shall be held responsible for the reports of test or analysis issued by the applicant.

(6) The testing of drugs or cosmetics, as the case may be, for identity, purity, quality and strength shall be carried out by persons whose qualifications and experience of testing are adequate in the opinion of the approving authority.

(7) The applicant shall provide books of standard recognised under the Provisions of the Act and the rules made thereunder and such books of reference as may be required in connection with the testing or analysis of the products for the testing of which approval is applied for.

Government Analysts

(1) The State Government may, by notification in the Official Gazette, appoint such persons as it thinks fit, having the prescribed qualifications, to be Government Analysts for such areas in the State and in respect of such drugs or [33](classes of drugs or such cosmetics or classes of cosmetics) as may be specified in the notification.

(2) The Central Government may also, by notification in the Official Gazette, appoint such persons as it thinks fit, having the prescribed qualifications to be Government Analysts in respect of such drugs or [34](classes of drugs or such cosmetics or classes of cosmetics) as may be specified in the notification.

(3) Notwithstanding anything contained in sub-section 91) or sub-section (2), neither the Central Government nor a State Government shall appoint as a Government Analyst any official not serving under it without the previous consent of the Government under which he is serving.

(4) No person who has any financial interest in the import, manufacture or sale of drugs or cosmetics shall be

appointed to be a Government Analyst under sub-section (1) or sub-section (2) of this section.

Inspectors

(1) The Central Government or a State Government may, by notification in the Official Gazette, appoint such persons as it thinks fit, having the prescribed qualifications, to be Inspectors for such areas as may be assigned to them by the Central Government or the State Government, as the case may be.

(2) The powers which may be exercised by an Inspector and the duties which may be performed by him, the drugs or [classes of drugs or cosmetics or classes of cosmetics] in relation to which and the conditions, limitations or restrictions subject to which, such powers and duties may be exercised or performed shall be such as may be prescribed.

(3) No person who has any financial interest [37][in the import, manufacture or sale of drugs or cosmetics] shall be appointed to be an Inspector under this section.

(4) Every Inspector shall be deemed to be a public servant within the meaning of Section 21 of the Indian Penal Code (45 of 1860), and shall be officially subordinate to such authority [38][having the prescribed qualifications,] as the Government appointing him may specify in this behalf.]

Powers of Inspectors.—(1) Subject to the provision of Section 23 and of any rules made by the Central Government in this behalf, an Inspector may, within the local limits of the area for which he is appointed.–

(i) inspect.

(a) any premises wherein any drug or cosmetic is being manufactured and the means employed for standardising and testing the drug or cosmetic;

(b) any premises wherein any drug or cosmetic is being sold, or stocked or exhibited or offered for sale, or distributed;

(ii) take samples of any drug or cosmetic.–

(a) which is being manufactured or being sold or is stocked or exhibited or offered for sale, or is being distributed:

(b) from any person who is in the course of conveying, delivering or preparing to deliver such drug or cosmetic to a purchaser or a consignee;

(iii) at all reasonable times, with such assistance, if any, as he considers necessary,–

(a) search any person, who, he has reason to believe, has secreted about his person, any drug or cosmetic in respect of which an offence under this Chapter has been, or is being, committed; or

(b) enter and search any place in which he has reason to believe that an offence under this Chapter has been, or is being, committed; or

(c) stop and search any vehicle, vessel or other conveyance which, he has reason to believe,is being used for carrying any drug or cosmetic in respect of which an offence under this Chapter has been, or is being, committed and order in writing the person in possession of the drug or cosmetic in respect of which the offence has been, or is being, committed, not to dispose of any stock of such drug or cosmetic for a specified period not exceeding twenty days, or, unless the alleged offence is such that the defect may be removed by the possessor of the drug of cosmetic, seize the stock of such drug or cosmetic and any substance or article by means of which the offence has been, or is being, committed or which may be employed for the commission of such offence;)

(cc) examine any record, register, document or any other material object found [42](With any person, or in any place, vehicle, vessel or other conveyance referred to in cluse (c)], and seize the same if this has reason to believe that it may furnish evidence of the commission of an offence punishable under this Act or the rules made thereunder;]

(ccc) require any person to produce any record, register or other document relating to the manufacture for sale or for distribution, stocking, exhibition for sale, offer for sale or distribution of any drug or cosmetic in respect of which he has reason to believe that an offence under this Chapter has been, or is being, committed;]

(iv) exercise such other powers as may be necessary for carrying out the purposes of this Chapter on any rules made thereunder.

(2) The provision of the [Code of Criminal Procedure, 1973 (2 of 1974)]. shall, so far as may be, apply to any search or seizure under this Chapter as they apply to any search or seizure made under the authority of a warrant issued under [45][Section 94] of the said Code.

[(2-A) Every record, register or other document seized under clause *(cc)* or produced under clause *(cca)* shall be returned to the person, from whom they were seized to who produce the same, within a period of twenty days of the date of such seizure or production, as the case may be, after copies thereof or extracts therefrom certified by that person, in such manner as may be prescribed, have been taken.]

(3) If any person wilfully obstructs an Inspector in the exercise of the powers conferred upon him by or under this Chapter, [47][or refuses to produce any record, register or other document when so required under clause *(cca)* of sub-section (1)] he shall be punishable with imprisonment which may extend to three years, or with fine, or with both.]

Procedure of Inspectors.—(1) Where an Inspector takes any sample of a drug [or cosmetic] under this Chapter, he shall tender the fair price thereof and may acquire a written acknowledgement therefor.

(2) Where the price tendered under sub-section (1) is refused, or where the Inspector seizes the stock of any drug (or cosmetic) under clause *(c)* of Section 22, he shall tender a receipt therefor the prescribed form.

(3) Where an Inspector takes 2 sample of a drug (or cosmetic) for the purpose of test or analysis, he shall intimate such purpose in writing in the prescribed form to the person from whom he takes round, in the presence of such person unless he willfully absents himself, shall drive the sample into four portions and effectively seal and suitably mark the same was permit such person to add his own seal and mark to all or any of the portions sealed and marked :

Provided that where are drug (or cosmetic) is made up in containers of small volume, instead of devic a sample as aforesaid, the Inspector may, and if the drug [53](or cosmetic) be soon that it is likely to deteriorate or be otherwise damaged by exposure shall, take curee or four, as the case may be, of the said containers after suitably marking are same and, where necessary, sealing them.

(4) The Inspector shall restore one portion of a sample so divided or one container, as the case may be, to the person from whom he takes it, and shall retain the remainder and dispose of the same as follows–

(i) one portion or container he shall forthwith send to the Government Analyst for test or analysis;

(ii) the second he shall produce to the Court before which proceedings, if any, are instituted in respect of the drug (or cosmetic); and

(iii) the third, where taken, he shall send to the person, if any, whose name, address and other particulars have been disclosed under Section 18-A.)

(5) Where an Inspector takes any action under clause (*c*) of Section 22,–

(I) he shall use all despatch in ascertaining whether

or not the drug (or cosmetic) contravenes any of the provisions of Section 18 and, if it is ascertained that the drug (or cosmetic) does not so contravene, forthwith revoke the order passed under the said clause or, as the case may be, take such action as may be necessary for the return of the stock seized; an institution or testing laboratory approved for the purposary the appointing authority, or

(ii) possesses a post-graduate degree in medicine or science pharmacy or pharmaceutical chemistry of a (University established in India by the law or has an equivalent qualification recognised and notified by the Central Government for such purpose) or possesses the Associatested Diploma of the Institution of Chemists (India) obtained by passing the said examination with 'Analysis of Drugs and Pharmaceuticals' as one of the subjects and has had after obtaining the said post-graduate degree or diploma not less than three years, experience in the testing of drugs in a laboratory, under the control of *(i)* a Government Analyst appointed under the Act or *(ii)* the head of an institution or testing laboratory approved for the purpose by the appointing authority:

Provided that :

(a) for the purpose of examination of items in Schedule C, the person appointed under clause (*a*) or clause *(b)* should be able to produce evidence of satisfactory training in physiology, bacteriology or serology or pathology or pharmacology or microbiology and should have experience of testing of the said items, in an institution or testing laboratory approved by the appointing authority, for a period of not less than five years in the case of a person appointed under clause *(a)* and of not less than three years in the case of a person appointed under clause *(b)*;

(b) for a period of four years from the date on which Chapter IV of the Act takes effect in the States, persons, whose training and experience are regarded by the appointing authority as affording subject to such further training, if any, as may be considered necessary, a reasonable guarantee of adequate knowledge and competence may be appointed as Government Analysts. The persons so appointed may, if the appointing authority so desires, continue in service after the expiry of the said period of four years;

(c) no person who is engaged directly or indirectly in any trade or business connected with the manufacture of drugs shall be appointed as a Government Analyst for any area:

Provided further that for the purpose of examination of Antisera. Toxoid and Vaccinesw and Diagnostic Antigens for Venterinary use, the person appointed shall be a person who is a graduate in Veterinary Science, or general science, or medicine or pharmacy and has had not less than five years' experience in the standardisation of biological products or a person holding a post-graduate degree in Veterinary Science, or general science, or medicine or pharmacy or pharmaceutical chemistry with an experience of not less than three years in the standardisation of biological products.

Provided also that persons, already appointed as Government Analysts may continue to remain in service, if the appointing authority so desires, notwithstanding the fact that they do not fullfil the qualifications as laid down in clause *(a)* clause *(b)* or the preceding proviso.

Duties of Government Analysts.—(1) The Government Analyst shall cause to be analysed or tested such samples of drugs and cosmetics as may be sent to him by Inspectors or other persons under the provisions of Chapter IV of the Act and shall furnish reports of the results of test or analysis in accordance with these Rules.

(2) A Government Analyst shall from time to time forward to the Government reports giving the result of analyti-

cal work and research with a view to their publication at the discretion of Government.

Procedure on receipt of sample—On receipt of a package from an Inspector containing a sample for test or analysis, the Government Analyst shall compare the seals on the packet with the specimen impression received separately and shall note the condition of the seals on the package. After the test or analysis has been completed, he shall forthwith supply to the Inspector a report in triplicate in Form 13 of the result of the test or analysis, together with full protocols of the test or analysis applied.

Explanation–It shall be deemed to be full and sufficient complance with the requirement of the rule in respect of the supply of "protocols of the tests or analysis applied", if–

(1) for pharmacopoeial drug, where the tests or methods of analysis prescribed in the official pharmacopoeia are followed, references to the specific tests or analysis in the pharmacopoeias are given in the report;

(2) for patent or proprietary medicines for which the tests and methods prescribed in any of the official pharmacopoeias are applicable and are followed, references to the specific tests or analysis in the pharmacopoeias are given in the report;

(3) for patent or proprietary medicines containing pharmacopoeial drugs for which the official tests or analysis or methods of essays are modified and applied, a description of the actual tests or, as the case may be analysis or methods of assays so applied is given in the report;

(4) for patent or proprietary medicines for which no pharmacopoeal test or methods of analysis are available or can be applied but for which tests or methods of analysis given in standard books or journals are followed, a description of such tests or methods of analysis applied together with the reference to the relevant books or jour-

nals from which the tests or methods of analysis have been adopted, is given in the report;

(5) for those drugs for which methods of test are not available and have been evolved by the Government Analyst, a description of tests applied is given in the report.]

[6]**Report of result of test or analysis**—An application from a purchaser for test or analysis of a drug under Section 26 of the Act shall be made in Form 14-A and the report of test or analysis of the drug made on such application shall be supplied to the applicant in Form 14-B.

Fee—The fees to be paid by a person submitting to the Government Analysist Under Section 26 of the Act for test or analysis of a drug [or cosmetic] purchased by him shall be those specified in Schedule B.

Qualifications of Inspectors—A person who is appointed an Inspector under the Act shall be a person who has a degree in Pharmacy or Pharmaceutical Sciences or Medicine with specialisation in Clinical Pharmacology or Microbiology from a University established in India by law:

Provided that only those Inspectors:-

(i) who have not less that 18 months' experience in the manufacture of at least one of the substances specified in Schedule C, or

(ii) who have not less than 18 month's experience in testing of at least one of the substances in Schedule C in a Laboratory approved for this purpose by the licensing authority, or

(iii) who have gained experience of not less than three years in the inspection of firms manufacturing any of the substances specified in Schedule C during the tenure of their services as Drugs Inspectors;

Shall be authorised to inspect the manufacture of the substances mentioned in Schedule C.]

Qualification of a Licensing Authority—No person shall be qualified to be a Licensing Authority under the Act unless :-

(i) he has graduate in Pharmacy or Pharmaceutical Chemistry or in Medicine with specialisation in Clinical Pharmacology or Microbiology from a University established in India by law; and

(ii) he has experience in the manufacture or testing of drugs or enforcement of the provisions of the Act for a minimum period of five years:

(1) Provided that the requirements as to the academic qualification shall not apply to those Inspectors and the Government Analysts who were holding those positions on the 12th day of April, 1989.

(2) All Inspectors appointed by the State Government shall be under the control of an officer appointed on this behalf by the State Government.

(3) For the purpose of these rules an officer appointed by the Central Government under sub-rule (1), or as the case may be, an officer appointed by the State Government under sub-rule (2), shall be a controlling authority.

Qualification of a Controlling authority— No person shall be qualified to be a Controlling Authority under the Act unless :-

(i) he is a graduate in Pharmacy or Pharmaceutical Chemistry or in Medicine with specialisation in Clinical Pharmacology or Microbiology from a University established in India by law; and

(ii) he has experience in the manufacture or testing of durgs of enforcement of the provisions of the Act for a minimum period of five years:

[Provided that the requirements as to the academic qualification shall not apply those Inspector and the Government Analysts who were holding those positions on the 12th day of April, 1989.]

Duties of Inspectors of premises licensed for sale— Subject to the instructions of the controlling authority, it shall be the duty of an Inspector authorized to inspect premises licensed for the sale of drugs–

(1) to inspect not less than twice a year all establishments licensed for the sale of drugs within the area assigned to him;

(2) to satisfy himself that the conditions of the licences are being observed;

(3) to procure and send for test or analysis, if necessary, imported packags which he has reason to suspect contain drugs being sold or stocked or exhibited for sale in contravention of the provisions of the Act or Rules thereunder;

(4) to investigate any complaint in writing which may be made to him;

(5) to institute prosecutions in respect of breaches of the Act and Rules thereunder;

(6) to maintain a record of all inspections made and action taken by him in the performance of his duties, including the taking of samples and the seizure of stocks, and to submit copies of such record to the controlling authority;

(7) to make such enquiries and inspections as may be necessary to detect the sale of drugs in contravention of the Act;

(8) when so authorized by the State Government, to detain imported packages which he has reason to suspect contain drugs, the import of which is prohibited.

Duties of Inspectors especially authorized to inspect the manufacture of drugs—Subject to the instructions of the controlling authority it shall be the duty of an Inspector authorized to inspect the manufacture of drugs–

(1) to inspect not less than twice a year, all premises licensed for manufacture of drugs within the area allotted to him and to satisfy himself that the conditions of the licence and provisions of the Act and Rules thereunder are being observed;

(2) in the case of establishments licensed to manufacture products specified in Schedules C are C(1) to inspect the plant and the process of manufacture, the means employed for standing and testing the drug, the methods and place of storage, the technical qualifications of the staff employed and all details of location, construction and administration of the establishment likely to affect the potency or purity of the product;

(3) to send forthwith to the controlling authority after each inspection a detailed report indicating the conditions of the licence and provisions of Act and Rules thereunder which are being observed and the conditions and provisions if any, which are not being observed;

(4) to take samples of the drug manufactured on the premises and send them for test or analyses in accordance with these rules;

(5) to institute prosecutions in respect of breaches of the Act and Rules thereunder.

IMPORT OF DRUGS

The following classes of drugs are prohibited to be imported into India :

(i) Misbranded drugs and misbranded cosmetics.

(ii) Drugs which do not comply with standards prescribed for them in the Act.

(iii) Drugs which claim to prevent or cure any of the diseases or ailments specified in Schedule J to the Rules.

(iv) Adultrated drugs harmful substance or toxic material which makes them injurious to health or admixed with any substance which reduce their qualities or strength.

(v) Spurious drugs and spurious cosmetics.

(vi) Drugs whose manufacture, sale and distribution are prohibited in the country of origin, except when they are required for the purpose of examination, test and analysis.

(vii) Patent and proprietary medicines whose true formula is not disclosed or cosmetic.

(viii) Any other drug whose import is prohibited under the Rules.

(ix) Drugs not having therapeutic values.

(x) Drugs containing ingredients in such quantities that there is no therapeutic justification.

(xi) Any cosmetic containing any ingredient which may render it unsafe or harmful for use under the directions indicated or recommended.

The following classes of drugs can be imported under a licence or permit granted by proper authority :

(a) All drugs specified in Schedule C and C1.

(b) Drugs specified in Schedule X.

(c) Small quantities of drugs imported for the purpose of examination, test and analysis.

(d) Drugs imported for personal use covered by a prescription of a Registered Medical Practitioner.

(e) Any new drug.

The licence remains valid upto December 31 of the following year in which it was granted, unless suspended or cancelled earlier. In the event of any changes in the constitution of a licensed firm, the licencee should inform the licensing authority accordingly.

When a single manufacturer abroad has more then one factory situated different places a separate import licence is required in respect of drugs manufactured at each premises.

A. IMPORT OF SCHEDULE C AND C1 DRUGS

An import licence, obtainable on application to the proper licensing authority, is necessary for the import of all schedule C and C1 drugs. The licence for the import of schedule

C and C1 drugs is granted subject to the following conditions:

(a) Licencee must have facilities for the storage of imported drugs so that the proportion of the drugs would be preserved.

(b) Licencee must maintain a record of the sale of imported drugs showing the particulars of the names of drugs and of the persons to whom they have been sold.

(c) Licencee must allow an inspector to inspect the premises whose imported drugs are stocked to check the records maintained in respect of their sale and purchase, to inspect any means employed to test the potency of the drugs and to take their samples for check analysis.

(d) Licencee must on request furnish to the licensing authority samples of drugs from all batches or from such batches as the licensing authority may direct together with full details of the tests, if any, carried out by the licencee.

(e) Licencee must not sell drugs from any batch from which samples have been furnished to the licensing authority in case he is so advised by the said authority. He may, however, dispose the batch when a certificate has been issued to him by the licensing authority authorizing him to sell the drugs from the batch. In case the licencee is informed by the licensing authority that any drug does not comply with the prescribed standards, he should recall that batch from the sales as far as possible.

(f) The licencee must comply with the undertaking given in from 9 and with such further requirements as may be specified and of which he has been given not less then four month's notice by the licensing authority.

The import licence may be suspended or cancelled by the licensing authority in respect of all drugs or certain specified drugs, if the licencee or the manufacturer fails to observe any of the conditions of the licence, after giving him an opportunity of explaining himself. Persons aggrieved by the decision of the licensing authority may appeal to a court of law written three months of the date of order whose decision shall be final.

B. IMPORT OF SCHEDULE X DRUGS

A licence is necessary for the import of Schedule X drugs. Before granting the licence the licensing authority must ensure that the licencee has proper facilities for storage of drugs and may also enquire into the occupation, trade or business ordinarily carried out by the applicants. The licensing authority may also refuse to grant the licence if the licence granted previously to the applicant was suspended or cancelled or in case the applicant failed to comply with any provisions of the Act and Rules or has been convicted under the Drugs and Cosmetics Act or the Narcotic and Psychotropic Substances Act. However, a person aggrieved by such decisions may appeal to the Central Government within 30 days whose decision shall be final.

C. IMPORT OF SMALL QUANTITIES OF DRUGS FOR EXAMINATION, TEST OR ANALYSIS

A licence is necessary for the import of small quantities of drugs for analytical purposes. The application for the licence is required to be made to the licensing authority, duly signed by the Head of the Institution where the drugs are to be used. The licensing authority has the right to call for such further particulars as may be considered necessary before the issue of the licence to the prospective applicant. The licence is issued subject to the following conditions :

(i) The licencee must use imported drugs exclusively for the purpose which they are imported and at places specified in the licence. The licensing authority may, however, authorize their use in any other place.

(ii) The licencee must keep a record of the substances imported under the licence with respect to their quantities, names of the manufacturers and the dates of their import and make report of the details to the licensing authority.

(iii) The licencee must allow an inspector to enter and inspect the premises where the imported drugs are kept, to check the records, to investigate the manners in which the drugs are being used and to take samples thereof for check analysis.

(iv) Licencee must comply with such further conditions as may be prescribed and of which he has been given at least one month's notice by the licensing authority. If the licencee fails to observe any of the conditions of the licence the same may be cancelled by the licensing authority. The licencee, however, has the right of appeal to the Central Government within three months of the date of such cancellation.

D. IMPORT OF DRUGS FOR PERSONAL USE

In the normal course small quantities of drugs (upto 100 average doses) whose import is otherwise prohibited, may be imported without any permit, provided they form part of passenger's bonafide luggage, are meant for his or her exclusive personal use and are declared to the Customs Authorities. (In case of exceptional circumstances import of the drugs in excess of 100 doses may be sanctioned by the Customs Authority). If the drugs are imported for personal use and otherwise then as a part of passenger's luggage a permit is necessary to cover the import. The permit is granted by the licensing authority, if the authority is satisfied that (a) the drugs is for bonafide personal use and (b) the quantity sought to be imported is reasonable and is covered by a prescription of a Registered Medical Practitioner.

E. IMPORT OF NEW DRUGS

No new drugs are allowed to be imported into the country without the sanction of the licensing authority in writing. All drugs whose composition is not recognized as safe for the use by experts and which have not been used to any large extent or for any appreciable period of time are to be regarded as New Drugs. Any patent or proprietary medicine containing any new drugs is also to be classed as new drug.

Permission for the import of new drugs may be obtained from the licensing authority after furnishing to him documentary evidence of the standards of quality, purity and strength of the drug. The application for import of new drugs including their fixed dose combinations should be accompanied by data specified in Schedule Y, provided that data on clinical trials for a drug may not be submitted, if the licensing authority decides to grant import permission without it in public interest.

SOME OTHER PROVISIONS REGARDING IMPORT OF DRUGS

Customs Collectors' authority over import

The law relating to goods whose import is prohibited Under Section 18 of the Sea Customs Act 1878 is applicable to drugs whose import is prohibited. The Customs Collector can detain any consignment of drugs whose import is prohibited and can report to the Drugs Controller of India. Samples of any drug whose standards are suspected or whose compliance with the Act and Rules is in doubt can be sent to Central Drugs Laboratory or any other laboratory specified for analysis and report.

The consignments from which samples have been drawn and sent for analysis may be detained by Customs Controller until receipt of reports on analysis.

If the report of the analysis indicates that the sample of any drug in the consignment does not come up to the prescribed standards or contravenes any of the provisions of Chapter III of the Act and Rules in any manner and the defects are such that they cannot be remedied by the importer, the Customs Collector may ask the importer to export the consignment back to the manufacturer within two months of the receipt of information from the Customs Collector or forfeit it to the Central Government for destruction.

PLACES WHERE DRUGS CAN BE IMPORTED

Import of drugs in India is allowed only through the following places :

Route	*Places*
By Sea	Madras, Bombay, Calcutta, Cochin and Visakhapatnam.
By Air	Madras, Bombay, Calcutta, Delhi and Ahmedabad.
By Rail	Ferozepur Cantt. and Amritsar Rly. Stations (in respect of drugs coming from Pakistan), Ranaghat, Bongegaon and Mahaiarsan Rly. Stations (in respect of drugs coming from Bangla Desh).

OFFENCES AND PENELTIES RELATED TO IMPORT OF DRUGS

Anyone who imports a spurious or adulterated drug or drugs which involve any risks to the human beings or animals or drugs not having claimed therapeutic values shall be punished with imprisonment up to three years or fine up to Rs. 5,000/- on first conviction and imprisonment up to five years and fine up to Rs. 10,000/- for the subsequent offence.

Persons importing drugs in contravention of other provisions are punishable with imprisonment up to six months and/or fine up to Rs. 500 on first conviction and imprisonment up to one year and/or fine up to Rs. 1000 on any subsequent conviction. These punishments shall be in addition to any punishment that may be imposed under the Sea Customs Act. The offences cannot the tried in courts inferior to that of a Metropolitan Magistrate or Judicial Magistrate of the First Class.

Drugs Exempt from Import Provisions class of Drugs	*Extent and conditions of exemption*
Drugs not intended for medicinal use.	Can be imported without any restriction provided their containers are labelled to indicate the fact that they are not intended for medicinal use.
Drugs in Schedule C required for manufacturing purposes and not	No licence required for import when imported by persons holding

	a licence for the manufacture of Schedule C and C1 Drugs.
Substances which are both drugs and articles of food such as condensed and powdered milk, malted fortified or otherwise : Lactose, Farex, Oats and other similar cereel preparation whether fortified or not, except those intended for parenteral administration.	
Virol, Bovnil, Chicken assence and other similar spices and condiments other than those which are of official quality.	Exempt from all import regulations.
Ginger, pepper, cumin, cinnamon and other similar spices and other than those which are of official quality.	

5

DRUGS AND MAGIC REMEDIES (OBJECTIONABLE ADVERTISEMENT ACT AND RULES)

INTRODUCTION

The means of advertising through which one introduces his products and relevent services to the users has become an essential part of the trade. Even the doctor and lawyers are advertising themselves to the public, the employers advertise jobs, the job-seekers have to advertise their expertise and qualifications in particular fields alongwith their educational qualifications. Similarly some institutes give advertisements regarding courses of study. The matrimonial advertisements are also eagrly awaited in leading newspapers or through marriage bureaus. Advertisement has become a common feature in our day-to-day life and a modern way of introducing newly manufactured items or goods to the society or in the market. But ethical and scientifically produced advertisements help the society while unethical or mischievous ones are very dangerous. Hence it is necessary to control them and save the public from their bad effects.

NEED OF THE ACT

Advertisements of ordinary consumer goods and that of drugs have a fundamental difference. The former are directed to the public or a consumer, the latter are meant for medical, para-medical and pharmaceutical professionals and not addressed to the public. This is because the use of drugs and medicines. On account of their therapeutic potencies and toxic effects need a lot of discretion and judgement in their use, which a lay man cannot exercise. To advertise the use of drugs directly to the public may lead to self-medication which may prove disastrous. The drugs should reach a patient through a competent doctor or a physician. This becomes imperative all the more, to control advertisements relating to the drugs and medicines. The attractive methods and magic remedies, in addition to the remedies for venereal diseases and sexual disorders, are openly advertised. Such type of advertisements have reached an alarming proportions, misleading the people in indulging self-medication and resorting to quacks whose only interests are in minting money through unfair means.

The Drugs and Magic (Objectionable Advertisements) Act was enacted to prohibit certain types of advertisements relating to drugs and magic remedies which make false claims and are likely to mislead public.

The prohibitions imposed by the Act, however, do not apply to the advertisements released through a bonafide scientific view, such as advertisements meant for medical practitioners and chemists or the advertisements made on behalf of the Governments of the respective States or the Central Government.

This Act is operational in the entire country except the State of Jammu and Kashmir. It came in force on April 1, 1955.

DEFINITIONS

The drugs and magic remedies advertisements are defined in the Act as follows :

(i) Advertisements : are defined to include all notices, circulars, labels, wrappers or other documents and also all announcement made orally or by means of producing or transmitting light, sound or smoke.

(ii) Drugs : are defined to include substances intended for the diagnosis, cure, mitigation, preparation or treatment of diseases in human beings or animals or for altering any structure or functions of the body of human beings or animals excepting articles of food.

Be it noted that the definition of drugs in this Act is different in many aspects from the definition of drugs in the Drugs and Cosmetics Act. For example the insect repellants, insecticides which kill insects causing diseases in human beings etc. which are deemed to be drugs in the Drugs and Cosmetics Act are not drugs under this Act.

(iii) Magic Remedies : are defined to include 'talisman', 'mantras', 'kavachas' and the same type of substances or attractions and charms of any kind which purport to possess miraculous powers of prevention or cure of diseases or of affecting or altering any type of functions of the bodies of human beings or animals.

(iv) Taking part in the publication of any advertisements : includes (a) the printing of the advertisements (b) the publication of any advertisement out side the territories to which this Act extends by or at the instance of a person residing within the said territories.

PROHIBITED ADVERTISEMENTS

The following types of advertisements are prohibited to be made under the Act :

(i) The advertisements, relating to drugs, which are likely to lead to their use in the following ailments or conditions :

   (a) For procurement of miscarriage or prevention of conception in women;

   (b) For the correction of menstrual disorders in women;

(c) For the maintenance or improvement of the capacity of human beings for sexual pleasure;

(d) For the diagnosis, prevention or cure of appendicitis, arterioseleosis, blindness, blood poisoning, brights' disease, cancer, cataract, deafness, diabetes, diseases and disorders and disorders of hair, optical system and uterus, disorders of menstrual flow, nervous system and prostatic glands, dropsy, epilepsy, female diseases (in general), fevers (in general), fits, form and structure of female bust, gall stones, kidney stones and bladder stones, gangrene, glaucoma, goitre, heart diseases, high or low blood pressure, hydrocele, hysteria, infantile, paralysis, insanity, leprosy, leucoderma, lockjaw, locomotor ataxia, lupus, nervous debility, obesity, plague, pleurisy, pneusnosia, rheumatism, ruptures, sexual impotence, smallpox, stature of persons, sterilitis in women, trachoma, tuberculosis, tumours, typhoid, ulcers of the gastro-intestinal tract, venereal diseases including syphlis, gonorrhoea, soft chancre, veneral granuloma and lymphogranuloma. (this list can be further amended to include such ailments requiring timely treatment in consultation with medical practitioners (registered).

(ii) Direct or indirect advertisements which give false impression regarding the real character of the drug or make any fake claims for it or are otherwise false or deceptive.

(iii) Advertisements which directly or indirectly, carry false impressions relating to magic remedies claiming their efficacy for any of the conditions outlines in (i) by persons, who purport to carry on the profession of administering magic remedies.

However, the prohibitions imposed on advertisements do not cover the following :

(a) Signboards or notices displayed by Registered Medical Practitioners on their premises indicating that treatment is undertaken for the diseases or disorders, advertisements relating to which are otherwise prohibited;

(b) Books or other materials, dealing with any matter relating to the diseases or ailments which are otherwise prohibited to be advertised, provided published from bonafide scientific or social stand-point;

(c) Advertisements regarding drugs which are sent confidentially, in the prescribed manner, to Registered Medical Practitioners. The advertisements are deemed to have been confidentially if they are sent by post bearing the words on top, in a conspicuous manner : "For the use of Registered Medical Practitioners."

(d) Advertisements relating to drugs printed or published by the Government or by any other agency, with the prior permission of the Governments should apply to the officers authorized on this behalf by the State or Central Governments stating the registered name and trade mark of the drug and special reasons justifying the sanction of the authorities concerned.

(e) Advertisements, labels or sets of instructions which are permitted under the Drugs and Cosmetics Act or Rules made thereunder.

Further, if the Central Government feels that the advertisements of any drug, which is otherwise prohibited under the Act, shall be in the interest of the public, it may permit its advertisement by a notification in the Official Gazette. In a recent notification the following classes of advertisements have also been exempted from the provisions of the Act provided the conditions noted against them are complied with :

ADVERTISEMENTS EXEMPTED ARE

(i) Leaflets or literature accompanying packings of drugs; or advertisements of drugs in medical, pharmaceutical, scientific and technical journals.

(ii) Price lists or therapeutic indexes published by manufacturers, importers or distributers of drugs duly licensed under the Drugs and Cosmetics Act, 1940 and the rules thereunder, or medical literature distributed by medical representatives representing manufacturers, importers or distributers of drugs, duly licensed under the Drugs and Cosmetics Act, 1940 and the rules thereunder.

CONDITIONS FOR EXEMPTION

The advertisement carries only such information as is needed for the guidance of registered medical practitioners in respect of matters relating to (a) therapeutic indications of the drugs, (b) its administration, (c) its dosages, (d) its side effects and (e) the precautions to be taken in treatment with the drug. The advertiser shall be held responsible to prove any claim made in the advertisement in respect of the drug is not false, exaggerated or misleading. The distribution of such literature is confined only to the Registered Medical Practitioners, hospitals, medical and research institutions, and chemists and druggists or pharmacy duly licensed and the provisions of the Drugs and Cosmetics Act and Rules.

PROHIBITION ON IMPORT AND EXPORT OF ADVERTISEMENTS

Some advertisements deemed to be goods whose export and import are prohibited under Section 19 of the Sea Customs Act, 1878, and all the provisions of that Act apply to these classes of advertisements outlined as above. An officer of the Central Government authorized in this respect may detain any consignment containing documents or advertisements prohibited under the Act. The importer or exporter after getting the detention of consignment will have to give an undertaking not to dispose of the consignment without the consent of the Customs Collector and return it to him when asked to do so within ten days of the notice, the customs collector may make over the consignment to the importer or the exporter.

OFFENCES AND PENALTIES

Who ever contravenes any of the provisions of this Act or Rules is liable to punishment with imprisonment up to six months or with fine or both on first conviction, and imprisoned up to one year or fine or both on any subsequent conviction.

If the contravention of this Act is committed by a company, every person who, at the time the offence was committed, was in charge of, and responsible to run and conduct its business, as well as the company, shall be deemed to be guilty and punished accordingly, unless it is proved that the offence was committed without his knowledge or that he has exercised due diligence to prevent the occurrence of that offence. If it is proved that the offence by a company was committed with connivance of, or is attributable to any neglect on the part of, any Director, Manager, Secretary etc. of the company, such person shall also be deemed to be guilty of that offence and shall be punished accordingly.

Where a person is convicted under this Act, the court may direct the forefeiture of any document, article or a thing, in respect of which the contravention is committed including the contents thereof.

6

NARCOTIC DRUGS AND PSYCHOTROPIC SUBSTANCES ACT, 1985[1]

(16 September, 1985)

An Act to consolidate and amend the law relating to narcotic drugs, to make stringent provisions for the control and regulation of operations relating to narcotic drugs and psychotropic substances and for matters connected therewith.

Be it enacted by Parliament in the Thirty-sixth Year of the Republic of India as follows:-

Preliminary

1. Short title, extent and commencement—(I) This Act may be called the Narcotic Drugs and Psychotropic

Substances Act, 1985.

(2) It extends to the whole of India.

2. Definitions—In this Act, unless the context otherwise requires;

(i) "addict" means a person addicted to any narcotic drug or psychotropic substance;

(ii) "Board" means the Central Board of Excise and customs constituted under the Central Boards of Revenue Act, 1963 (54 of 1963);

(iii) "cannabis (hemp)" means—

(a) *charas,* that is, the separated resin, in whatever form, whether crude or purified, obtained from the cannabis plant and also includes concentrated preparation and resin known as hashish oil or liquid hashish;

(b) *ganja,* that its, the flowering or fruiting tops of the cannabis plant (excluding the seeds and leaves when not accompanied by the tops), by whatever name they may be known or designated; and

(c) any mixture, with or without any neutral material, of any of the above forms of cannabis or any drink prepared therefrom.

(iv) "cannabis plant" means any plant of the genus cannabis;

(v) "coca derivative" means—

(a) crude cocaine, that is, any extract of coca leaf which can be used, directly or indirectly, for the manufacture of cocaine;

(b) ecgonine and all the derivatives of ecgonine from which it can be recovered;

(*c*) cocaine, that is, methyl ester of benzoly-ecgonine and its salts; and

(d) all preparations containing more than 0.1 per cent of cocaine;

(vi) "coca leaf" means–

(a) the leaf of the coca plant except a leaf from which all ecgonine, cocaine and any other ecgonine alkaloids have been removed;

(b) any mixture thereof with or without any neutral material, but does not include any preparation containing not more than 0.1 per cent of cocaine;

(vii) "coca plant" means the plant of any species of the genus Exythroxylon;

(viii) "conveyance" means a conveyance of any description what-soever and includes any aircraft, vehicle or vessel;

(ix) "manufacture", in relation to narcotic drugs or psychtropic substances, includes–

(a) all processes other than production by which such drugs or substances may be obtained;

(b) refining of such drugs or substances;

(c) transformation of such drugs or substances; and

(d) making of preparation (otherwise than in a pharmacy on prescription) with or containing such drugs or substances;

(x) "manufactured drug " means–

(a) all coca derivatives, medicinal cannabis, opium derivatives and popply straw concentrate;

(b) any other narcotic substance or preparation which the Central Government may, having regard to the available information as to its nature or to a decision, if any, under any. International Convention, by notification in the Official Gazette, declare to be a manufactured drug,

but does not include any narcotic substance or preparation which the Central Government may, having regard to the available information as to its nature or to a decision, if any, under any International Convention, by notification in the Official Gazette, declare not to be a manufactured drug;

(xi) "medicinal cannabis", that is, medicinal hemp, means any extract or tincture of cannabis (hemp);

(xii) "Narcotics Commissioner" means the Narcotics Commissioner appointed under Section 5;

(xiii) "narcotic drug" means coca leaf, cannabis (hemp), opium, poppy straw and includes all manufactured drugs;

(xiv) "opium" means–

(a) the coagulated juice of the opium poppy ; and

(b) any mixture, with or without any natural material, of the coagulated juice of the opium poppy,

but does not include any preparation containing not more than 0.2 per cent of morphine;

(xv) "opium derivative" means–

(a) medicinal opium, is, opium, which has undergone the processes necessary to adapt it for medicinal use in accordance with the requirements of the Indian Pharmacopoeia or any other pharmacopoeia notified in this behalf by the Central Government, whether in powder form or granulated or otherwise or mixed with neutral materials;

(b) prepared opium, that is, any product of opium obtained by any series of operations designed to transform opium into an extract suitable for smoking and the dross or other residue remaining after opium is smoked;

(c) phenanthrene alkaloids, namely, morphine, codeine, the-baine and their salts;

(d) diacetylmorphine, that is, the alkaliodalso known as dia morphine or heroin and its salt; and

(e) all preparations containing more than 0.2 per cent of morphine or containing any diacetylmorphine;

(xvi) "opium poppy" means–

(a) the plant of the species *Papaver* somniferum L.; and

(b) the plant of any other species of *Papaver* from which opium or any phenanthrene alkaloid can be extracted and which the Central Government may, by notification in the Official Gazette, declare to be opium poppy for the purposes of this Act;

(xvii) "poppy straw" means all parts (except the seeds) of the opium poppy after harvesting whether in their original form or cut, crushed or powdered and whether or not juice has been extracted therefrom;

(xviii) "poppy straw concentrate" means the material arising when poppy straw has centered into a process for the concentration of its alkaloids;

(xix) "preparation", in relation to a narcotic drug or psychotropic substance means any one or more such drugs or substances in dosage form or any solution or mixture, in whatever physical state, containing one or more such drugs or substances;

(xx) "prescribed" means prescribed by rules made under this Act;

(xxi) "production" means the separation of opium, poppy straw, coca leaves or cannabis from the plants from which they are obtained;

(xxii) "psychotropic substance" means any substance, natural or synthetic, or any natural material or any salt or preparation of such substance or material included in the list of psychotropic substances specified in the Schedule;

(xxiii) "to import inter-State" means to bring into a State or Union territory in India from another State or Union territory in India;

(xxiv) "to import into India", with its grammatical variations and cognate expressions, means to bring into India from a place outside India and includes the bringing into any port or airport or place in India of a narcotic drug or a psychotropic substance intended to be taken out of India without being removed from the vessel, aircraft, vehicle or any other conveyance in which it is being carried.

3. Power to add or omit from the list of psychotropic substances The Central Government may, if satisfied that it is necessary or expedient to do so on the basis of–

(a) the information and evidence which has become available to it with respect of the nature and effects of, and the abuse or the scope for abuse of, any substance (natural or synthetic) or natural material or any salt or preparation, of such substance or material; and

(b) the modifications or provisions (if any) which have been made to, or in, any International Convention with respect to such substance, natural material or salt or preparation of such substance or material.

By notification in the Official Gazette, add to, or, as the case may be, omit from, the list of psychotropic substances specified in the Schedule such substance or natural material or salt or preparation of such substance or material.

Authorities and officers

Central Government to take measures for preventing and combating abuse of and illicit traffic in narcotic drugs, etc–(1) Subject to the provisions of this Act, the Central Government shall take all such measures as it deems necessary or expedient for the purpose of preventing and combating abuse of narcotic drugs and psychotropic substances and the illicit traffic therein :

(i) coordination of actions by various officers, State Governments and other authorities;

(ii) obligations under the Internatioal Conventions;

(iii) assistance to the concerned authorities in foreign countries and concerned international organizations with a view to facilitating coordination and universal action for prevention and suppression of illicit traffic in narcotic drugs and psychotropic substances;

(iv) identification, treatment, education, after care, rehabilitation and social re-integration of addicts;

(v) such other matters as the Central Government deems necessary or expedient for the purpose of securing the effective implementation of the provisions of this Act and preventing and combating the abuse of narcotic drugs and psychotropic substances and illicit traffic therein.

Officers of Central Government–(1) Central Government shall appoint a Narcotics Commissioner and may also appoint such other officers with such designations as it thinks fit for the purposes of this Act.

(2) The Narcotics Commissioner shall, either by himself or through officers subordinate to him, exercise all powers and perform all functions relating to the superintendence of the cultivation of the opium poopy and production of opium and shall also exercise and perform such other powers and functions as may be entrusted to him by the Central Government.

(3) The officers appointed under sub-section (1) shall be subject to the general control and direction of the Central Government, or, if so directed by that Government, also of the Board or any other authority or officer.

The Narcotic Drugs and Psychotropic Substances Consultative Committee–(1) The Central Government may constitute, by notification in the Official Gazette, an advisory committee to be called "The Narcotic Drugs and Psychotropic Substances Consultative Committee" (hereafter in this section referred to as the Committee) to advise the Central Government on such matters relating to the administration of this Act as are referred to it by that Government from time to time.

(2) The Committee shall consist of a Chairman and such other members, not exceeding twenty, as may be appointed by the Central Government.

(3) The Committee shall meet when required to do so by the Central Government and shall have power to regulate its own procedure.

(4) The Committee may, if it deems it necessary to do so for the efficient discharge of any of its functions, constitute one or more sub-committees and may appoint to any such sub-committee, whether generally or for the consideration of any particular matter, any person (including a non-official) who is not a member of the Committee.

(5) The term of office of, the manner of filling casual vacancies in the officers of and the allowances, if any, payable to the Chairman and other members of the Committee, and the conditions and restrictions subject to which the Committee may appoint a person who is not a member of the Committee as a member of any of its sub-committees, shall be such as may be prescribed by rules made by the Central Government.

7. Officers of State Government–(1) The State Government may appoint such officers with such designations as it thinks fit for the purposes of this Act.

(2) The officers appointed under sub-section (1) shall be subject to the general control and direction of the State Government, or, if so directed by that Government, also of any other authority or officer.

PROHIBITION, CONTROL AND REGULATION

8. Prohibition of certain operations–No person shall—

(i) cultivate any coca plant or gather any portion of coca plant; or

(ii) cultivate the opium poppy or any cannabis plant; or

(iii) produce, manufacture, possess, sell, purchase, transport, ware-house, use, consume, import inter-State, export inter-State, import into India, export from India or tranship any narcotic drug or psychotropic substance,

except for medical or scientific purposes and in the manner and to the extent provided by the provisions of this Act or the rules or orders made thereunder and in a case where any such provision, imposes any requirement by way of licence, permit or authorisation also in accordance with the terms and conditions of such licence, permit or authorisation:

A. Power of Central Government to permit, control and regulate—(1) Subject to the provisions of Section 8, the Central Government may, by rules–

permit and regulate–

(i) the cultivation, or gathering of any portion (such cultivation or gathering being only on account of the Central Government) of coca plant, or the production, possession, sale, purchase, transport, import inter-State, export inter-State, use or consumption of coca leaves;

(ii) the cultivation (such cultivation being only on account of Central Government) of the opium poppy;

(iii) the production and manufacture of opium and production of poppy straw;

(iv) the sale of opium and opium derivatives from the Central Government factories for export from India or sale to State Government or to manufacturing chemists;

(v) the manufacture of manufactured drugs (other than prepared opium) but not including manufacture of medicinal opium or any preparation containing any manufactured drug from materials which the maker is lawfully entitled to possess;

(vi) the manufacture, possession, transport, import inter-State, export inter-State, sale, purchase, consumption or use of psychotropic substances;

(vii) the import into India and export from India and transhipment of narcotic drugs and psychotropic substances;

B. Power of State Government to permit, control and regulate–(1) Subject to the provisions of Sections of Section 8, the State Government may, by rules–

(i) permit and regulate–

(a) the possession, transport, import inter-State, export inter-State, warehousing, sale, purchase, consumption and use of poppy straw;

(b) the possession, transport, import inter-State, export inter-State, sale, purchase, consumption and use of opium;

(c) the cultivation of any cannabis plant, production, manufacture, possession, transport, import inter-State, export inter-State, sale, purchase, consumption or use of cannabis (excluding *charas)*;

(d) the manufacture of medicinal opium or any preparation containing any manufactured drug from materials which the maker is lawfully entitled to possess;

(e) the possession, transport, purchase, sale, import inter-State, export inter-State, use or consumption of manufactured drugs other than prepared opium and of coca leaf and any preparation containing any manufactured drug;

(f) the manufacture and possession of prepared opium from opium lawfully possessed by an addict registered with the State Government on medical advice for his personal consumption.

Offences and penalties

Punishment for contravention in relation to poppy straw—Who ever, in contravention of any provision of this Act or any rule or order made or condition of a licence granted thereunder, produces, possesses, transports, imports inter-State, exports inter-State, sells purchases, uses or ommits to warehouse poppy straw, shall be punishable with rigorous imprisonment for a term which shall not be less than ten years but which may extend to twenty years and shall also be liable to fine which shall not be less than one lakh rupees but which may extend to two lakh rupees:

Provided that the court may, for reasons to be recorded in the judgement, impose a fine exceeding two lakh rupees.

Punishment for contravention in relation to coca plant and coca leaces.—Whoever, in contravention of any provision of this Act or any rule or order made or condition of licence granted thereunder manufactures, possesses, sells, purchases, transports, imports inter-State, exports inter-State or uses prepared opium shall be punishable with rigorious imprisonment for a term which shall not be less than ten years but which may extend to twenty years and shall also be liable to fine which shall not be less than one lakh rupees but which may extend to two lakh rupees:

Provided that the court may, for reasons to be recorded in the judgement, impose a fine exceeding two lakh rupees.

Punishment for embezzlement of opium by cultivator—Any cultivator licensed to cultivate the opium poppy on account of the Central Government who embezzles or otherwise illegally disposes of the opium produced or any part thereof, shall be punishable with rigorous imprisonment for a term which shall not be less than ten years by which may extend to twenty years and shall also be liable to fine which shall not be less than one lakh rupees but which may extend to two lakh rupees.

Provided that the court may, for reasons to be recorded in the judgment, impose a fine exceeding two lakh rupees.

Punishment for contravention in relation to cannabis plant and cannabis—Whoever, in contravention of any provision of this Act or any rule or order made or condition of licence granted thereunder–

(i) cultivates any cannabis plant; or

(ii) produces, manufactures, possesses, sells, purchases, transports, imports inter-State, exports inter-State or uses cannabis.

shall be punishable,–

(i) where such contravention relates to *ganja* or the cultivation of cannabis plant, with rigorous imprisonment for a term which may extend to five years and shall also be liable to fine which may extend to fifty thousand rupees;

(ii) where such contravention relates to cannabis other than *ganja,* with rigorous imprisonment for a term which shall not be less than ten years but which may extend to twenty years and shall also be liable to fine which shall not be less than one lakh rupees and which may extend to two lakh rupees.

Provided that the court may, for reasons to be recorded in the judgment, impose a fine exceeding two lakh rupees.

Punishment for contravention in relation to manufactured drugs and preparations—Whoever, in contravention of any provision of this Act, or any rule or order made or condition of licence granted there-under manufactures, possesses, sells, purchases, transports, imports inter-State, exports inter-State or uses any manufactured drug or any preparation containing any manufactured drug shall be punishable with rigorous imprisonment for a term which shall not be less than ten years but which may extend to twenty years and shall also be liable to fine which shall not be less than one lakh rupees but which may extend to two lakh rupees.

Provided that the court may, for reasons to be recorded in th judgment, impose a fine exceeding two lakh rupees.

Punishment for contravention in relation to psychotropic substances—Whoever, incontravention of any provision of this Act or any rule or order made or condition of licence granted thereunder, manufactures, possesses, sells purchases, transports, Imports Inter-State, exports inter-State, or uses any psychotropic substance shall be punishable with rigorous imprisonment for a term which shall not be less than ten years but which may extend to twenty years and shall also be liable to fine which shall not be less than one lakh rupees but which may extend to two lakh rupees.

Provided that the court may, for reasons to be recorded in the judgment, impose a fine exceeding two lakh rupees

Punishment for illegal import into India, export from India or transhipment of narcotic drugs and psychotropic substances—Whoever, in contravention of any provision of this Act or any rule or order made or condition of licence or permit granted or certificate or authorisation issued thereunder, imports into India or exports from India or tranships any narcotic drug or psychotropic substance shall be punishable with rigorous imprisonment for a term which shall not be less than ten years but which may extend to twenty years and shall also be liable to fine which shall not be less than one lakh rupees but may extend to two lakh rupees.

Provided that the court may, for reasons to be recorded in the judgment, impose a fine exceeding two lakh rupees.

Punishment for external dealings in narcotic drugs and psychotropic substances in contravention of Section 12—Whoever engages in or controls any trade whereby a narcotic drug or a psychotropic substance is obtained outside India and supplied to any person outside India without the previous authorisation of the Central Government or otherwise than in accordance with the conditions (if any) of such authorisation granted under Section 12, shall be punishable with rigorous imprisonment for a term which shall not be less than ten years but which may extend to twenty years and shall also be liable to fine which shall not be less than one lakh rupees but may extend to two lakh rupees.

Provided that the court may, for reasons to be recorded in the judgment, impose a fine exceeding two lakh rupees.

Punishment for allowing premises, etc., to be used for commission of an offence—Whoever, being the owner or occupier or having the control or use of any house, room, enclosure, space, place, animal or conveyance, knowingly permits it to be used for the commission by any other person of an offence punishable under any provision of this Act, shall be punishable with rigorous imprisonment for a term which shall not be less than ten years but which may extend to twenty years and shall also be liable to fine which shall not be less than one lakh rupees but which may extend to two lakh rupees.

Provided that the court may, for reasons to be recorded in the judgment, impose a fine exceeding two lakh rupees.

THE SCHEDULE

List of Psychotropic Substances

Sl. No.	International non-proprietary names	Other non-proprietary names	Chemical name
1	2	3	4
1		DEP	N, N-Diethyltryptamine
2		DMHP	3-(1, 2-Dimethylheptyl)-1-hydroxy-7, 8, 9, 10-tetrahydro-6, 9-trimethyl-6H-dibenzo (b,d) pyran
3		DMP	N, N-Dimethyltryptamine
4	(+)-LYSERGIDE	LSD-25	(+)-N, N-Diethyllysergamide (d-lysergic acid diethylamide)
5		mescaline	3, 4, 5-Trimethoxyphenethylamine
6		parahexyl	3-Hexyl-1-hydrosxy-7, 8, 9, 10-tetrahydro-6, 6, 9-trimethyl-6H-dibenzo (b, d) pyran
7	ETICYCLIDINE	PGE	N-Ethyl-1-phenylcyclohexylamine
8	ROLICYCLIDINE	PHP, PCPY	1-(1-Phenylcyclohexyl) pyrrolidine
9		psilocine, psilotsin	3-(2-Dimethylaminoethyl)-4hydroxyindole
10	PSILOCYBINE		3-(2-Dimethylaminoethyl)-indol-4-yl dihydrogen phosphate
11		STP, DOM	2-Amino-1-(2, 5-dimethoxy-4-methyl) phenylpropane
12	TENOCYCLIDINE	TCP	1-[1-(2Thienyl) cyclohexyl] piperidine

Sl. No.	International non-proprietary names	Other non-proprietary names	Chemical name
1	2	3	4
13		THC	Tetrahydrocannabinols, the following isomers: D 6a (10a), D 6a (7), D 7, D 8, D 9, D 10, D 9(11) and their stereochemical varinats
14		DOB	2, 5-dimethoxy-4-bromoamphetamine
15		MDA	3, 4-methylenedioxyamphetamine
16	AMPHETAMINE		(±)-2-Amino-1-phenylpropane
17	DEXAMPHETAMINE		(+)-2-Amino-1-phenylpropane
18	MECLOQUALONE		3-(0-Chlorophenyl)-2-methyl-4(3H)-quinazolinone
19	METHAMPHETAMINE		(+)-2-Methylamino-1-phenylpropane
20	METHAQUALONE		2-Methyl-3-0-tolyl-4 (3H)-quinazoinone
21	METHYLPHENIDATE		2-Phenyl-2(2-piperidyl) acetic acid, methyl ester
22	PHENCYCLIDINE	PCP	1-(1-Phenylcyclohexyl) piperidine
23	PHENMETRAZINF		3-Methyl-2-phenylmorpholine
24	AMOBARBITAL		5-Tthyl-5(3-methylbutyl) barbitutic acid
25	CYCLOBARBITAL		5-(1-Cyclohexen-1-yl)-5ethylbarbitric acid
26	GLUTETHIMIDE		2-Ethyl-2-phenylglutarimide
27	PENTAZOCINE		1, 2, 3, 4, 5, 6-Hexahydro-6, 11-dimethyl-3-(3-methyl-2-butenyl-2, 6-methano-3-benzazocin-8-01
28	PENTOBARBITAL		5-Ethyl-5-(1-methylbutyl) barbituric acid
29	SECOBARBITAL		5-Allyl-5-(1-methylbutyl) barbituric acid
30	ALPRAZOLAM		8-Chloro-1-methyl-6-phenyl-4H-s-triazolo (4, 3-a) (1, 4) benzodiazepine
31	AMFEPRAMONE		2-(Diethylamino) propiophenone
32	BARBITAL		5, 5-Diethylbarbitutic acid

Sl. No.	International non-proprietary names	Other non-proprietary names	Chemical name
1	2	3	4
33	BENZPHETAMINE		N-Benzyl-N, a -dimethylphenethylamine
34	BROMAZEPAM		7-Bromo-1, 3-dihydro-5(2-pyridyl)-2H-1, 4-benzo diazepin-2-one
35	CAMAZEPAM		7-Chloro-1, 3-dihydro-5-(2-pydroxy-1-methyl-5-phenyl 2-H-1, 4-benzodiazepin-2-one dimethylcarbamate (ester)
36	CHLORDIAZEPOXIDE		7-Chloro-2-(methylamino)-5-phenyl-3H-1, 4-benzodiazepine-4-oxide
37	CLOBAZAM		7-Chloro-1-methyl-5-phenyl-1H-1, 5-benzodiazepine-2, 4 (3H, 5H)-dione
38	CLONAZEPAM		5-(0-Chlorophenyl)-1, 3-dihydro-7-nitro-2H-1, 4-benzodiazepin-2-one
39	CLORAZEPATE		7-Chloro-2, 3-dihydro-2-oxo-5-phenyl-1H, 4-benzodiazepine-3-carboxylic acid
40	CLOTIAZEPAM		5-(0-Chlorophenyl)-7-ethyl-1, 3-dihydro-1-methyl-2H-thieno (2, 3-e)-1, 4-diazepin-2-one
41	CLOXAZOLAM		10-Chloro-11 b-(0-chlorophenyl)-2, 3, 7, 11b-tetrahydrooxazolo-(3-2-d) (1, 4) benzodiazepine-6 (5H)-one
42	DELORAZEPAM		7-Chloro-5-(0-chlorophenyl)-1, 3-dihydro-2H-1, 4-benzodiazepin-2-one
43	DIAEPAM		7-Chloro-1, 3-dihydro-1-methyl-5phenyl-2H-1, 4-benzodiazepin-2-one
44	ESTAZOLAM		8-Chloro-6-phenyl-4H-s-triazolo (4, 3-a) (1, 4) benzodiazepine
45	ETHCHLORVYNOL		Ethyl-2-chlorovinylethynylcarbinol
46	ETHINAMATE		1-Ethynylcyclohexanolcarnamate
47	ETHYLLOFLAZEPATE		Ethyl 7-chloro-5-(0-fluorophenyl)-2, 3-dihydro-2oxo-1H-1, 4-benzociazepine-3-carboxylate

Sl. No.	International non-proprietary names	Other non-proprietary names	Chemical name
1	2	3	4
48	FLUDIAZEPAM		7-Chloro-5-(0-fluorophenyl)-1, 3-dihydro-1-methyl-2H-1, 4-benzodiazepin-2-one
49	FLUNITRAZEPAM		5-(0-Fluorophenyl)-1, 3-dihydro-1-methyl-7-nitro-2H-1, 4-benzodiazepin-2-one
50	FLURAZEPAM		7-Chloro-1-[2-(diethylamino) ethyl]-5-(0-fluorophenyl)-1, 3-dihydro-2H-1, 4-benzodiazepin-2-one
51	HALAZEPAM		7-Chloro-1, 3-dihydro-5-phenyl-1-(2, 2, 2-trifluoroethyl)-2H-1, 4-benzodiazepine-2-one
52	HALOXAZOLAM		10-Bromo-11b-(o-fluorophenyl)-2, 3, 7, 11btetrahydrooxazolo [3, 2-d] [1, 4]-benzodiazepin-6 (5h)-one
53	KETAZOLAM		11-Chloro8-, 12b-dihydro-2, 8-dimethyl-12b-phenyl-4H-[1, 3]-oxazino-[3, 2-d] [1, 4] benzodiazepine-4, 7(6H)-dione
54	LEFETAMINE	SPA	(--)-1-Dimethylamino-1, 2-diphenylethane
55	LOPRAZOLAM		6-(0-Chlorophenyl)-2, 4-dihydro-2-[(4-methyl-1-piperazinyl) methylene]-8-nitro-1H-imidazo [1, 2-a] [1, 4] benzodiazepin-1-one
56	LORAZEPAM		7-Chloro-5-(0-chlorophenyl)-1, 3-dihydro-droxy-2H-1, 4-benzodizaepin-2-one
57	LORMETAZEPAM		7-Chloro-5-(0-chlorophenyl)-1, 3-dihydro-droxy-2H-1, 4-benzodiaxepin-2-one
58	Mazindol		5-(p-Chlorophenyl)-2, 5-dihydro-3H-imidazo [2, 1-x] isoindol-5-01
59	MEDAZEPAM		7-Chloro-2, 3-dihydro-1-methyl-5-phenyl-1H-1, 4-benzodiazepine
60	MEPROBAMATE		2-Methyl-2-proply-1, 3-propanediol dicarbamate

Sl. No.	International non-proprietary names	Other non-proprietary names	Chemical name
1	2	3	4
61	METHYLPHENO-BARBITAL		5-Ethyl-1-methyl-5phenylbarbituric acid
62	METHPRYLON		3, 3-Diethyl-5-methyl-2, 4-piperidine-
63	NIMETAZEPAM		1, 3-Dihydro-7-nitro-5-phenyl-2H-1, 4-benzodiazepine-2-one
64	NITRAZEPAM		1, 3-Dihydro-7-nitro-5-phenyl-2H-1, 4-benzodiazepin-2-one
65	NORDAZEPAM		7-Chloro-1, 3-dihydro-5-phenyl-1-(2H)-1, 4-benzodiazepin-2-one
66	OXAZEPAM		7-Chloro-1, 3-dihydro-3-hydroxy-5-phenyl-2H-1, 4-benzodiazepine-2-one
67	OXAZOLAM		10-Chloro-2, 3, 7, 11b-tetrahydro-2-methyl-11b-phenyl-oxazolo (3, 2-d) (1, 4) benzodiaepin-6 (5H)-one
68	PHENDIMETRAZINE		(+)-3, 4-Dimethyl-2-phenylmorpholine
69	PHENOBARBITAL		5-Ethyl-5-phenylbarbitutic acid
70	PHENTERMINE		<, a-Dimethylphenethylamine
71	PINAZEPAM		7-Chloro-1, 3-dihydro-5-pheny-1-(2-propynyl)-2H-1, 4-benzodiazepin-2-one
72	PIPRADROL		1, 1-Diphenyl-1-(2-piperidyl)-methanol
73	PRAZEPAM		7-Chloro-1-(cyclopropylmethyl-1), 3-dihydro-5-phenyl-2H-1, 4-benzodiazepin-2-one
74	TEMAZEPAM		7-Chloro-1, 3-dihydro-3-hydroxy-1-methyl-5-phenyl-2H-1, 4-benzodiazepin-2-one
75	TETRAZEPAM		7-Chloro-5-(cycloexen-1-yl)-1-, 3-dihydro-1-methyl-2H-1, 4-benzodiazepin-2-one
76	TRIAZOLAM		8-Chloro-6- (0-chlorophenyl)-1-methyl-4H-S-triazolo (4, 3-a) (1, 4) benzodiazepine
77	Salts and Preparations of above.		

7

DRUGS (PRICES CONTROL) ORDER 1995

S.O. 18(E)-In exercise of the powers confered by section 3 of the Essential Commodities Act, 1955 (10 of 1955), the Central Government hereby makes the following order, namely:-

1. Short title and commencement—(1) This order may be called the Drugs (Prices Control) Order, 1995.

(2) It shall come into force on the date of its publication in the Official Gazette.

2. Definitions--In this order, unless the context otherwise requires–

(i) "bulk drug" means any pharmaceutical, chemical biological or plant product including its salts, esters, stereo-isomers and derivatives, conforming to pharmacopoeial or other standards speficied in the Second Schedule to the Drugs and Cosmetics Act, 1940 (23 of 1940), on which is used as such or as an ingredient in any formulation;

(ii) "capital employed" means net fixed assests plus

working capital of a manufacturer in relation to manufacture of bulk drugs;

(iii) "ceiling price" means a price fixed by the Government for Scheduled formulations in accordance with the provisions of paragraph 9;

(iv) "dealer" means a person carrying on the business of purchase or sale of drugs, whether as a wholesaler or retailer and whether or not in conjunction with any other business, and includes his agent;

(v) "distributor" means a distributor of drugs or his agent or a stockist appointed by a manufacturer or an importer for stocking his drugs for sale to a dealer;

(vi) "drug" include—

(a) all medicines for internal or external use of human beings or animals an all substances intended to be used for, or in the diagnosis treatment, mitigation, or prevention of any disease or disorder in human beings or animals, including preparations applied on human body for the purpose of repelling insects like mosquitoes;

(b) such substances, intended to effect the structure or any function of the human or animal body or intended to be used for the destruction of vermin or insects which cause disease in human beings or animals, as may be specified from time to time by the Government by Notification in the Official Gazette, and

(c) bulk drugs and formulations:

(vii) "Form" means a form specified in the second Schedule;

(viii) "formulation" means a medicine processed out of, or containing one or more bulk drug or drugs with or without the use of any Pharmaceutical aids, for internal or external use for or in the diagnosis, treatment, migitation and prevention of disease in human beings or animals, but shall not include–

(a) any medicine included in any bonafide Ayurvedic (including Sidha) or Unani (Tibb) systems of medicines;

(b) any medicine included in the Homoeopathic system of medicine; and

(c) any substance to which the provisions of the Drugs and Cosmetics Act, 1940 (23 of 1940) do not apply;

(ix) "free reserve" means a reserve created by appropriation of profits, but does not include reserves provided for contingent liability, disputed claims, goodwill, revaluaio and other similar reserves;

(x) "Government" means the Central Government;

(xi) "import" with its grammatical variations and cognate expressions means bringing into India from a place outside India, and "importer" in relation to any goods at any time between their importation and consumption, includes any owner or any person holding himself out to be the importer;

(xii) "manufacture" in relation to any drug, includes any process or part of a process for making, altering, finishing, packing, labelling, breaking or otherwise treating or adapting any drug with a view to its sale and distribution, but does not include the compounding or dispensing of any drug or the packing of any drug in the ordinary course of retail business, and "to manufacture" shall be made accordingly;

(xiii) "manufacturer" means any person who manufactures a drug;

(xiv) "net-worth" means the paid-up share capital of

a company plus free reserve, if any, and surpluses excluding outside investments which are not readily available for operational activity;

(xv) "non-Scheduled bulk drug" means a bulk drug not specified in the First Schedule;

(xvi) "non-Scheduled formulation" means a formulation not containing any bulk drug specified in the First Schedule;

(xvii) "Pre-tax return" means Profit before payment of income tax and surtax includes such other expenses as do not form part of the cost of formulation;

(xviii) "price list" means a price list referred to in paragraphs 14 and 15 and includes a supplementary price list;

(xix) "retail price" means the retail price of a drug arrived at or fixed in accordance with the provisions of this order and includes a ceiling price;

(xx) "retailer" means a dealer carrying on the retail business of sale of drugs to customers;

(xxi) "Scheduled bulk drug" means a bulk drug specified in the First Schedule;

(xxii) "Scheduled formulation" means a formulation containing any bulk drug specified in the First Schedule either individually or in combination with other drugs, including one or more that one drug or drugs not specified in the First Schedule except single ingredient formulation based on bulk drugs specified in the First Schedule and sold under the generic name;

(xxiii) "sale turn-over" means the product of units of formulations sold by a manufacturer or an importer, as the case may be in an accounting year multiplied by retail price inclusive of sales tax, if any, paid on direct sales by the manufacturer or importer, but does not include excise duty and local taxes, if any;

(xxiv) "Schedule" means a Schedule annexed to this Order;

(xxv) "wholesaler" means a dealer or his agent or a stockist appointed by a manufacturer or an importer for the sale of his drugs to a retailer, hospital, dispensary, medical, educational or research institution purchasing bulk quantities of drugs.

3. Power to fix the maximum sale prices of bulk drugs specified in the First Schedule--(i) The Government may, with a view to regulate the equitable distribution and increasing supplies of a bulk drug specified in the First Schedule and making it available at a fair price, from different manufacturers, after making such enquiry as it deems fit, fix from time to time, by notification in the Official Gazette, a maximum sale price at which such bulk drug shall be sold;

(ii) While fixing the maximum sale price of a bulk drug under sub-paragraph 91), the Government shall take into consideration a post-tax return of fourteen per cent on net worth or a return of twenty two per cent on capital employed or in respect of a new plant an internal rate of return of twelve per cent based on long term marginal costing depending upon the opition for any of the specified rates of return that may be exercised by the manufacturer of a bulk drug.

(iii) No person shall sell a bulk drug at a price exceeding the maximum sale price fixed under sub-paragraph (1) plus local taxes, if any.

Provided that until the price of a bulk drug is fixed by the Government under sub-paragraph (1), the price of such bulk drug shall be the price which prevailed immediately before the commencement of this Order and the manufacturer of such bulk drug shall not sell the bulk drug at a price exceeding the price prevailing immediately before the commencement of this Order.

(iv) Where, after the commencement of this Order, any manufacturer commences production of any bulk drug specified in the First Schedule, he shall within fifteen days of the commencement of production of such bulk drug, furnish the details to the Government in Form I, and any such additional information as may be required by the Government and the Government may after receipt of the information and after making such enquiry as it may deem fit, may fix the maximum sale price of bulk drug by notification in the Official Gazette.

(v) Any manufacturer, who desires revision of the maximum sale price of a bulk drug fixed under sub-paragraph (1) or (4) or as permissible under sub-paragraph (3), as the case may be, shall make an application to the Government in Form I and the Government shall after making such enquiry, as it deems fit within a period of four months from the date of receipt of the complete information, fix a revised price for such bulk drug or reject the application for revision for reasons to be recorded in writing.

4. Information to be furnished by the manufacturer in relation to the Scheduled bulk drugs—Every manufacturer, producing a Scheduled bulk drug shall furnish to the Government—

(i) a list of all Scheduled bulk drugs produced by him within thirty days of the commencement of this Order and indicate the details of the cost of each of such bulk drug in Form I;

(ii) the details of the cost of each Scheduled bulk drug produced by him, including such bulk drug which has been produced after the commencement of this Order, in Form I by the 30th September, every year.

5. Information to be furnished by the manufacturer in relation to the non-Scheduled bulk drugs--Every manufacturer, producing a non-Scheduled bulk drug shall furnish to the Government–

(i) a list of all such bulk drugs produced by him within thirty days of the commencement of this Order and indicate the details of the cost of each of such bulk drugs in Form II;

(ii) the details of the cost of each non-Scheduled bulk drug produced by him, including such bulk drug which has been produce after the commencement of this Order, in Form II;

Provided that, for the purpose of this paragraph, the Government, may after making such enquiry as it may deem necessary in public interest, fix or revise the price of any non-Scheduled bulk drug and the manufacturer or importer of such bulk drug shall not sell the such non-Scheduled bulk drugs at a price exceeding the price so fixed or revised, within fifteen days of receipt of the order.

6. Power to direct manufacturers for bulk drugs to sell bulk drugs to other manufacturers of formulations–(a) With a view to achieving adequate production and regulating the equitable distribution, the Government may, from time to time, by general or special order, direct any manufacturer of any bulk drug to sell such bulk drug to such other manufacturers of formulations as may be specified in such order.

Provided that while making any such order, the Government shall have regard to all or any of the following factors, namely:–

(i) the requirement for captive consumption of such manufacturer, and:

(ii) the requirement of other manfacturers.

(b) For the purpose of making any order under sub-paragraph (1), the Government may call for such information from manufacturer, importer or distributor, of bulk drugs, as it may consider necessary and such manufacturer, importer or distributor shall be bound to furnish such information within such time as may be specified by the Government.

7. Calculation of retail price of formulation--The retail price of a formulation shall be calculated by the Government in accordance with the following formula, namely:-

R.P. = (M C. + C.C + P. M. + P. C.) x (1 + MAPE/100) + E.D

where,–

"R.P." means Retail Price;

"M.C." means material cost and includes the cost of drugs and other pharmaceutical aids used including averages if any, plus process loss thereon specified as a norm from time to time by notification in the official Gazette on this behalf;

"C.C." means conversion cost worked out in accordance with established procedures of costing and shall be fixed as a norm every year by notification in the Official Gazette on this behalf;

"P.M." means cost of the packing material used in the packing of concerned formulation, including process loss, and shall be fixed as a norm every year by notification in the Official Gazette on this behalf;

"P.C." means packing charges worked out in accordance with established procedures of costing and shall be fixed as a norm every year by notification in the Official Gazette on this behalf;

"MAPE" (Maximum Allowable Post-manufacturing Expenses) means all costs incurred by a manufacturer from the stage of ex-factory cost to retailing and includes trade margin and margin for the manufacturer and it shall not exceed one hundred per cent for indigenously manufactured Scheduled formulations;

"E.D." means excise duty.

Provided that in case of an imported formulation, the landed cost shall form the basis for fixing its price alongwith such margin to cover selling and distribution expenses including interest and importer's profit which shall not exceed fifty per cent of the landed cost.

Explanation–For the purpose of this proviso, "landed cost" means the cost of import of formulation inclusive of customs duty and clearing charges.

8. Power to fix retail price of Scheduled Formulations—(i) The Government may, from time to time, by order, fix the retail price of a Scheduled formulation in accordance with the formula laid down in paragraph 7.

(ii) Where the Government fixes or revises the price of any bulk drug under the provision of this Order and a manufacturer utilises such bulk drug in his Scheduled formulations he shall, within thirty days of such fixation or revision, make an application to the Government, in Form-III for price revision of all such formulation and the Government may, if it considers necessary, fix or revise the price of such formulation.

(iii) The retail price of a formulation once fixed by the Government under sub-paragraphs (1) and (2) shall not be increased by any manufacturer except with the prior approval of the Government.

(iv) Any manufacturer, who desires revision of the retail price of a formulation fixed under sub-paragraph (1), shall make an application to the Government in Form III or Form I, as the case may be, and the Government shall after making such enquiry, as it deems fit within a period of two months from the date of receipt of the complete information, fix a revised price for such formulation or reject the application for revision for reasons to be recorded in writing.

(v) Notwithstanding anything contained in the foregoing sub-paragraphs, the retail price of a scheduled formulation, of a manufacturer shall, until the retail price thereof it fixed under the provisions of this Order, be the price which prevailed immediately before the commencement of this Order, and the manufacturer of such formulation shall not sell the formulation at a price exceeding the price prevailing immediately before the commencement of this Order.

(vi) No manufacturer or importer shall market a new pack, if not covered under sub-paragraph 3 of para 9, or a new formulation or a new dosage form of his existing Scheduled formulation without obtaining the prior approval of its price from the Government.

(vii) No person shall sell or dispose of any imported Scheduled formulation without obtaining the prior approval of its price from the Government.

9. Power to fix ceiling price of Scheduled formula-

tions—(i) Notwithstanding anything contained in this Order, the Government may, from time to time, by notification in official Gazette, fix the Ceiling Price of a scheduled formulation in accordance with the formula laid down in paragraph 7, keeping in view the cost or efficiency, or both, of major manufacturers of such formulations and price shall operate as the ceiling sale price for all such packs including those sold under generic name and for every manufacturer of such formulations.

(ii) The Government may, either on its own motion or on application made to it in this behalf by a manufacturer in Form III of IV, as the case may be, after calling for such information as it may consider necessary, by notification in the Official Gazette, fix a revised ceiling price for a Scheduled formulation.

(iii) With a view to enabling the manufacturers of similar formulations to sell those formulations in pack size different to the pack size for which ceiling price has been notified under the sub-paragraphs (1) and (2), manufacturers shall work out the price for their respective formulation packs in accordance with such norms, as may be notified by the Government, from time to time, and he shall intimate the price of formulation pack, so worked out, to the Government and such formulation packed shall be released for sale only after the expiry of sixty days of such intimation.

Provided that the Government may, if it considers necessary, by order revise the price so intimated by the manufacturer and upon such revision, the manufacturer shall not sell such formulation at a price exceeding the price so revised.

Explanation–For the purpose of this paragraph the "Scheduled formulation" includes single ingredient formulation based on bulk drugs specified in the First Schedule and sold under the generic name.

10. Power to revise price of bulk drugs and formulations-- Notwithstanding anything contained in this order:

(i) the Government may, after obtaining such informations as may be considered necessary from a manufacturer or importer, fix or revise the retail price of one or more formulations marked by such manufacturer or importer, including a non-Scheduled formulation, in such manner as the pre-tax return on the sales turnover of such manufacturer or importer does not exceed the maximum pre-tax return specified in the Third Schedule;

(ii) the Government may if it considers necessary to do so in public interest, after calling for such information by order fix or revise the retail price of any formulation including a non-Scheduled formulation;

(iii) the Government may, if it considers necessary to do so in public interest, by order include any bulk drug in the First Schedule and fix or revise the prices of such a bulk drug and formulations containing such a bulk drug in accordance with the provisions of paragraph 3, 7, 8 and 9 as the case may be.

11. Fixation of price under certain circumstances-- Where any manufacturer, importer of a bulk drug or formulation fails to submit the application for price fixation or revision, as the case may be, or to furnish information as required under this Order, within the time specified therein, the Government may, on the basis of such information as may be available with it, by order to fix a price in respect of such bulk drug or formulation as the case may be.

12. power to recover dues accured under the Drugs (Prices Control) Order, 1979 and to deposit the same into the Drugs Prices Equalisation Account—(i) Notwithstanding anything contained in this order, the Government may by notice, require the manufacturer, importer or distributor, as the case may be, to deposit the amount which has accured under the provisions of the Drugs (Prices Control) Order, 1979 on or before the commencement of this Order, into the Drugs Prices Equalisation Account and the manufacturer, importer or distributor, as the case may be, shall deposit the said amount into the said Account within such time as the Government may specify in the said notice.

(ii) The existing amount, if any, in the Drugs Prices Equalisation Account on or before the date of commencement of this Order, and the amount deposited under sub-paragraph (1) shall be utilised for–

(a) paying to the manufacturer, importer or distributor, as the case may be, the short-fall between his retention price and the common selling price or, as the case may be, the pooled price for the purpose of increasing the production, or securing the equitable distribution and availability at fair prices, of drugs;

(b) meeting the expenses incurred by the Government discharging the functions under this paragraph; and

(c) promoting higher education and research in Pharmaceutical Sciences and Technology and for the purposes incidental thereto.

13. Power to recover overcharged amount--Notwithstanding anything contained in this order, the Government shall by notice, require the manufacturers, importers or distributors as the case may be, to deposit the amount accured due to charging of prices higher than those fixed or notified by the Government under the provision of Drugs (Prices Control) Order, 1987 and under the provisions of this Order.

14. Carrying into effect the price fixed or revised by the Government, its display and proof thereof—(i) Every manufacturer or importer shall carry into effect the price of a bulk drug or formulation, as the case may be, as fixed by the Government from time to time, within fifteen days from the date of notification in the Official Gazette or receipt of the order of the Government on this behalf by such manufacturer or importer.

(ii) Every manufacturer, importer or distributor of a formulation intended for sale shall display in indelible print mark, on the label of container of the formulation and the minimum pack thereof offered for retail sale, the retail price of that formulation, notified in the Official Gazette or ordered by the Government in this behalf, with the words "retail price not to exceed" preceding, it, and "local taxes extra" succeeding it, in the case of Schedule formulations:

Provided that in the case of a container consisting of smaller saleable packs, the retail price of such smaller pack shall also be displayed on the label of each smaller pack and such price shall not be more than the pro-rata retail price of the main pack rounded off to the nearest paisa.

(iii) Every manufacturer or importer shall issue a price list and supplementary price list, if required, in Form V to the dealers, State Drugs Controllers and the Government indicating reference to such price fixation or revision as covered by the order or Gazette notification issued by the Government, from time to time.

(iv) Every retailer and dealer shall display the price list and the supplementary price list, if any, as furnished by the manufacturer or importer, on a conspicious part of the premises where he carries on business in a manner so as to be easily accessible to any person wishing to consult the same.

15. Display of prices of non-Scheduled formulations and price list thereof--(i) Every manufacturer, importer or distributor of a non-Scheduled formulation intended for sale shall display on indelible print mark, on the label of container of the formulation and the minimum pack thereof offered for retail sale the retail price of that formulation with the words "maximum retail price" preceding it and the words "inclusive of all taxes" succeeding it:

Provided that in the case of a container consisting of smaller saleable packs, the retail price of such smaller pack shall also be displayed on the label of each smaller pack and such prices shall not be more than the pro-rata retail price of the main pack rounded off to the nearest paisa.

(ii) Every manufacturer or importer shall issue a price list and supplementary price list, if required, of the non-Scheduled formulations in Form V to the dealers, State

Drugs Controllers and the Government indicating changes, from time to time.

(iii) Every retailer and dealer shall display the price list and the supplementary price list, if any, as furnished by the manufacturer or importer, on a conspicuous part of the premises where he carries on business in a manner so as to be easily accessible to any person wishing to consult the same.

16. Control of sale prices of bulk drugs and formulations—No person shall sell any bulk drug or formulation to any consumer at a price exceeding the price specified in the current price list or price indicated on the label of the container or pack thereof, whichever is less, plus excise duty and all local taxes, if any, payable in the case of Scheduled formulations and maximum retail price inclusive of all taxes in the case of non-Scheduled formulations.

17. Sale of split quantities of formulations—No dealer shall sell loose quantity of any formulation at a price which exceeds the pro-rata price of the formulation plus 5 per-cent thereof.

18. Manufacturer, distributor or dealer not to refuse sale of drug—Subject to the provisions of the Drug and Cosmetics Act, 1940 (23 of 1940) and the Rules framed thereunder—

(i) no manufacturer or distributor shall withhold from sale or refuse to sell to a dealer any drug without good and sufficient reasons;

(ii) no dealer shall withhold from sale or refuse to sell any drug available with him to a customer intending to purchase such drug.

19. Maintenance of records and production thereof for inspection—(i) Every manufacturer and importer shall maintain in such form as may be specified by the Government, records relating the sales turnover of individual bulk drugs manufactured or imported by him, as the case may be, and the sales turnover of formulations. Packwise and also such other records as may be directed from time to time by the Government and the Government shall have the power to call for such records or to inspect such records at the premises of the manufacturer or importer.

(ii) Every manufacturer or importer shall within six months of the close of the accounting year, submit to the Government information in respect of turnover and allocation of sales and expenses for that year in Form-VI.

(iii) Every dealer, manufacturer or importer shall maintain the cash memo or credit memo, books of account and records of purchase and sale of drugs and shall make available such records for inspection by the Government or any officer authorised on this behalf by the Government.

21. Power of entry, search and seizure—(i) Any Gazetted Officer of the Central Government or of a State Government authorised by a general or special order by the Central Government or, as the case may be, by the State Government in this behalf may, with a view to securing compliance with this Order or to satisfy himself that the provisions of this Order have been complied with–

(a) enter and search any place;

(b) seize any drug, alongwith the containers, packages or coverings in which the drug is found, in respect of which he suspects that any provision of this Order has been, is being, or is about to be contravened, and thereafter take all measures necessary for securing production of the drug, containers, packages or coverings, so seized, in a court of law and for their safe custody pending such production;

(c) seize any document, such as, cash memo or credit memo books, books of account and records of purchase and sale of the drugs in respect of which he suspects that any provision of thid Order has been, is being, or is about to be contravened.

(ii) The provision of section 100 of the Code of Criminal Procedure, 1973 (2 of 1974), relating to search and seizure shall, so far as may be apply to searches and seizures under this Order.

The First Schedule

(See Paragraph 2 and 3)

LIST OF BULK DRUGS

1. Sulphamethozazole
2. Penicillins
3. Tetracycline
4. Rifampicin
5. Streptomycin
6. Ranitidine
7. Vitamin 'C'
8. Betamethasone
9. Metronidazole
10. Chloroquine
11. Insulin
12. Erythromycin
13. Vitamin 'A'
14. Oxytetracycline
15. Prednisolone
16. Cephazolin
17. Methyldopa
18. Aspirin
19. Trimethoprim
20. Cloxacillin
21. Sulphadimidine
22 Salbutamol
23. Famotidine
24. Ibuprofen
25. Metamizol (analgin)
26. Doxycycline

27. Ciprofloxacin
28. Cefotaxime
29. Dexamethasone
30. Ephedrine
31. Vitamin B1 (Thiamine)
32. Carbamazepine
33. Vitamin B2 (Riboflavin)
34 Theophyline
35. Levodopa
36. Tolnaftate
37. Vitamin E
38. Nalidixic acid
39. Griseofulvin
40. Gentamicin
41. Dextropropoxyphene
42. Halogenated hydroxyquinoline
43. Pentazocine
44. Captopril
45. Naproxen
46. Pyrental
47. Sulphadoxine
48. Norafloxacin
49. Cefdrosyl
50. Panthonates & panthenols
51. Furazolidone
52. Pyrithioxine
53. Sulphadiazine
54. Framycetin
55. Verapamil
56. Amikacin sulphate

57. Glipizide
58. Spironolactone
59. Pentoxyfylline
60. Amodiaguin
61. Sulphamoxole
62. Frusemide
63. Pheniramine maleate
64. Chloroxyllenols
65. Becampicillin
66. Lincomycin
67. Chlorpropamide
68. Mebhydroline
69. Chlorpromazine
70. Methendienone
71. Phenyl butazone
70. Methendienone
71. Phenl butazone
72. Lynetranol
73. Salazosulphapyrine
74. Diosmine
75. Trimipramine
76. Mefenamic acid.

8

THE POISONS ACT

INTRODUCTION

Pharmaceutically it is a common problem of poisoning. Majority of the poisoning cases are either suicidal or accidental. A pharmacist should be thoroughly familiar with common poisons. He is required to know the effects of the poison and ability to combat them. Familiarity with the Poison Act and problems arising out of poisoning are a must for a pharmacist. Day in and day out people of social and common existence are dovens of medicaments, tranquillisers, or aspirin compounds, cyanide and certain household solvents or products containing them. Pharmacists should have complete knowledge of the Poison Act as detailed in this chapter. They should be fully conversant to combat the effects of poison on human beings.

THE POISON ACT

To regulate the storage, labelling and sale of poisons as well as to control their imports, the Poison Act was passed in 1919. This Act empowers the Central Government to regulate the import of poisons across any of the customs frontiers. Various State Governments have been authorised to frame rules for possession and sale of poisons. All substances specified as poisons are notified under the Poisons Act, and are deemed as poisons for the purpose of this Act. In exercising their duties the professionals of medicine or veterinary practitioners in good faith are not covered by this Act. The provisions of this Act are in additions to the rules framed for dispensing and sale of poisons under the Drugs and Cosmetics Act, 1940.

POWER OF THE STATE GOVERNMENT TO REGULATE THE POSSESSION FOR SALE AND SALE OF ANY POISON

The State Government may by rule regulate within the whole or any part of the territories under its administration the possession for sale and the sale, whether wholesale or retail, of any specified poison. Such rule may provide for:

(i) grant of licences to possess any specified poison for sale, wholesale or retail and fixing of the fee (if any) to be charged for such licences;

(ii) the classes of persons to whom alone such licences may be granted;

(iii) the classes of persons to whom alone any such poison may be sold;

(iv) the maximum quantity of any such poison which may be sold to any one person.

(v) the maintenance by vendors of any such poison of registers of sale, the particulars to be entered in such registers and the inspection of the same;

(vi) the safe custody of such poisons and the labelling of the vessels, packages or coverings in which, such poison is sold or possessed for sale and

(vii) the inspection and examination of any such poison when possessed for sale by any such vendor.

To regulate the possession and sale of poisons the State Governments are authorised to issue rules and notifications under Poisons Act. The licences may be granted to persons for a specified class of poisons under these rules. The quantity to be sold under pecified class of poisons to a person or persons is notified under the rules. The State Governments are found to make rules for the safe custody of poisons and labelling of vessels and covering etc. in which the poisons are sold or kept in the area wherever the sale of poisons are to be regulated. The States are also empowered to restrict sale of poisons or possession any specified poison where there are frequent cases using such poisons for murders or mischievous purposes or for poisoning the cattle.

IMPORT OF POISONS

Power to prohibit importation into India of any poison except under licence : The Central Government may by notification in the Official Gazette prohibit, except under and in accordance with the conditions of a licence, the importation into India across any customs frontier defined by the Central Government of any specified poison and may by rule-regulate the grant of licences.

The Central Government is the main authority to grant licence for import of poisons.

PENALTIES AND OFFENCES

A person under the Poison Act shall be liable for various kinds of penalties stiffer or mild considering the nature of offences committed by him.

Penalty for unlawful importation

— Commits a breach if any rule made under the section 2 of the Act.

— Imports without a licence into India across a customs frontier defined by the Central Government any poison. The importation of which is for the time being. restricted under section 3 of the Act.

— breaks any condition of a licence for the importation of any poison granted to him under section 3.

Shall be punishable

(i) on first conviction, with imprisonment for a term which may, entered to three months, or with fine which may entered to five hundred rupees or with both and

(ii) on a second or subsequent conviction with imprisonment for a term which may extend to six months or with five which may extend to 1000 rupees or with both.

ISSUE OF WARRANTS

The District Magistrate and Sub-Divisional Magistrate, and a Commissioner in a presidency town, is empowered to issue warrants of search where a contraband poison is kept or concealed. Under the Code of Criminal Procedure and in accordance with the warrants, the persons directed with the warrants are authorised to enter and search the suspected premises or places.

9

THE MEDICINAL AND TOILET PREPARATIONS (EXCISE-DUTY) ACT AND RULES

Alcohol is widely used for preparing medicines. It is indispensable for manufacture of medicines and toilet preparations. The alcohol used for medicinal preparations cannot be used as an ordinary alcoholic beverage and it is subject to lower rate of excise duty in comparision to that used either for drinking or for the manufacture of toilet goods like preparation of cosmetics.

The Act has helped in checking the menace of large scale interstate smuggling of medicinal preparations having alcohol because of different rates of excise duties in different states. This Act has rendered uniform rates of duties throughout the country.

Now under the authority of licence granted for the manufacture of spirituous and other narcotic preparations applicant holds the requisite licence for the manufacture of drugs. The powers, duties and responsibilities of various officers entrusted with the administration of the Act are also specified in the rules.

DEFINITIONS

1. **Alcohol :** means ethyl alcohol of any strength and purity having the chemical composition C_2H_5OH.
2. **Dutiable goods :** means the medicinal and toilet prepations specified in schedule as being subject to the duties of excise carried under the Act.
3. **Excise Officer :** means an Officer of Excise Department of any state and any person empowered to exercise all or any of the powers of the excise officer under this Act.
4. **Manufacture :** includes any process incidental to or ancillary to the completion of the manufacture of any dutiable goods.
5. **Medicinal Preparations :** includes all drugs which are a remedy or prescription prepared for internal or external use of human beings or animals and all substances intended to be used for or in the treatment, mitigation or prevention of disease in human beings or animals.
6. **Narcotic drug or Narcotic :** means a substance which is cocoa leaf, or cocoa derivative or opium or derivative of opium or Indian hemp and shall include any other substance capable of causing or producing in human beings dependence, tolerance, and withdrawal syndromes and which the Central Govt. may by notification in the official Gazette, declare to be narcotic drug or narcotic.
7. **Toilet preparations :** means any preparation which is intended for use in the toilet of the human body or in perfuming apparel of any description, or any substance intended to cleanse, improve, or alter the complexion, hair, skin and teeth, and includes deodorants and perfumes.
8. **Absolute alcohol :** means alcohol conforming to the British pharmacopeial specifications for dehydrated alcohol.
9. **Bonded manufactory :** means the premises

approved and licensed for the manufacture and storage of medicinal and toilet preparations containing alcohol, opium, Indian hemp or other narcotic drug on which duty has not been paid.

10. **Non-Bonded Manufactory** : means the premises approved and licensed for the manufacture and storage of medicinal and toilet preparations containing alcohol, opium, Indian hemp and other narcotic drug or narcotics on which duty has been paid.

11. **Denatured alcohol or denatured spirit** : means alcohol of any strength which has been rendered unfit for human consumption by the addition of substances approved by the Central Govt. or by State Govt. with approval of the Central Govt.

12. **Finished store** : means that portion of a non-bonded or bonded manufactory which is set apart for the storage of its finished preparations.

13. **Laboratory** : means that portion of a non bonded or bonded manufactory in which the actual manufacture of dutiable goods takes place.

14. **Rectified spirit** : means plain undenatured alcohol of a strength not less than 50.00 over proof and includes absolute alcohol.

15. **Spirit store** : means that portion of the bonded or non- bonded manufactory which is set apart for the storage of alcohol, opium, Indian hemp and other narcotic drugs or narcotics purchased free of duty or at prescribed rates of duty.

16. **Sub-standard preparation** : is (a) a Pharmaceutical preparation in which the amount of any of the various ingredients is below the minimum that the pharmacopoeial composition would require or (b) a proprietary medicine which does not conform to the formula or the test of ingredients disclosed on the label on the container or on the container.

17. **Standard preparation** : means a preparation other than a sub-standard preparation.

18. Unrestricted preparation : means any medicinal or toilet preparations containing alcohol but other than restricted preparation or a spurious preparation.

19. Warehouse : means any place or premises licensed under Rule 70.

MANUFACTURE IN BOND

(1) The manufacture of preparations containing alcohol, licence must be obtained. When the preparations are manufactured in a premises, licenced or approved for the purpose and the duty is not paid on them until the finished products are removed from these licensed premises, they are deemed to be manufactured in bond.

(2) A licence must be obtained from the excise commissioner of the concerned state where the business is proposed to be carried out by every person to engage himself in the above manufacture.

(3) At least 2 months before the proposed date of commencement of the manufacture, the application for the licence should be submitted on the proposed form together with prescribed fee and the particulars as the Act for example—

(i) Name and address of the applicant.

(ii) The amount of capital to be invested and full description of vats, stills and other permanent apparatus.

(iii) The approximate date of start of the production or the manufacture in a whole time or a part time.

(iv) The type and number of licences held by the applicant under the Drug and Cosmetics Act 1940 alongwith the list of preparations and product that he proposes to manufacture.

(v) the site and elevation plan of the laboratory building indicating there in the different doors, rooms and windows.

For each application submitted for licence, the following fees has to be paid.

	Rupee	Consumption of alcohal
(i)	Rs 100.00	Less than 4,000 L.P. Litres per annum.
(ii)	Rs 200.00	4,006 L.P. litres or more.
(iii)	Rs 25.00	Ayurvedic Unani medicine containing self generated alcohol.

The licensing authority shall fix the amount of security before granting the licence.

The licensing authority will see into following on receipt of the application :

(a) The technical personnel employed for the manufacture, their qualifications and previous experience.

(b) The equipment and machinery in the bonded laboratory.

(c) The proposed building of the bonded laboratory and its suitability.

(d) The financial position of the applicant and its soundness.

(i) For granting of licence if the excise commissioner is satisfied that the applicant is a fit person for the issue of a licence after the above enquiries, he should approve the plans of the buildings and equipment submitted to him and may direct issue the licence.

(ii) Licensing authority may verify the construction after its completion because the premises specified in the licence is only covered under its conditions.

(iii) A separate licence for each set of promises must be obtained if in a case a person has more than one place of business.

(iv) In case the licencee wishes to transfer his business to another person fresh licence should be obtained by the transferee.

(v) The licence must be got suitably amended & notified to the authority at least 10 days in advance if the licencee wishes to transfer the business to another premises.

(vi) The licence must be renewed after its validity of the year. At least one month before the commencement of the year the application must be submitted for removal with an additional fee equivalent to 25% of original fee.

(vii) If licencee fails to observe any condition of the licence or has been convicted of an offence under Section 109 or 116 of Indian penal code. The licencing penal may suspend or invoke a licence.

(viii) The excise commissioner or any other officer authorized by him should be allowed by the licencee to inspect his premises or goods for ordering the remarks of the visiting officer, A visit book, duly paged & stamped should be maintained by the licencee.

THE BONDED LABORATORY

It should include the following compartment

(i) A spirit store (until or unless it is attached to either a distillery or a spirit warehouse).

(ii) A place (room) for the maintenance of medicinal peparations.

(iii) One or more rooms for storage of finished medicinal peparations.

(iv) A separate manufacturing room and a separate room or rooms for the storage of finished toilet goods should be provided if the manufacturing of toilet preparation is also undertaken.

(v) For the excise official incharge of bonded laboratory accommodation with necessary furniture near the entrance should be provided.

REQUIREMENTS OF A BONDED LABORATORY

(a) It should have only one entrance with only one door for each compartment.

(b) The opening of the laboratory should be done in the presence of excise officer incharge. All doors should be securely closed with excise ticket locks in his absence.

(c) In the bonded premises every window should be provided with maleable iron rods of 1.7 cm in thickness set 10 cm apart and embodied in brickwork to a depth of 5 cm. They should be covered on the inside with a strong wire netting or expanded metal of a mesh not more than 2.5 cm in diameter or length.

(d) Each room in the laboratory should be provided with a board indicating therein its serial no. & purpose.

(e) The pipes from sinks inside the laboratory should be connected with a general drainage system of the premises.

(f) In order to cut off the supply of the gas and the electric current at the end of day's work, they should be arranged accordingly.

(g) For storage of alcohol and other narcotic drug received under bond, permanent vessel should be provided.

(h) A distinctive serial no and a statement of full capacity of the vessel intended for holding alcohol should be provided with each vessel.

(i) To show the content of each vessel tables should be constructed at 2.5 cm and at 2.5 mm.

(j) Excise ticket locks securing should be made to all vessels containing preparation on which duty has not been paid.

MANUFACTURING OF ALCOHOLIC PREPARATIONS

Following step is or adopted for manufacture of alcoholic preparation

(i) Obtaining of spirit from distillery or spirit warehouse : A distillary or spirit warehouse approved by the excise commissioner supplies the spirit for the manufacture of medicinal or toilet preperation on an indent in the prescribed form countersigned by the officer incharge of the lab. The requirement of spirit can be obtained by the manufacturer either from sources situated inside the same or in the other state.

No wastage of spirit during its transit from a distillery to a bonded lab is permitted. The manufacturer is liable to pay duty on any loss of amount of spirit, if some loss occurs due to negligence.

(ii) Verification and storage of spirit on its arrival and the bonded lab : The consignment of the spirit should be verified in volume $ strength by the excise officer who should enter the amount in the register maintained for the purpose. The spirit should be stored after verification.

(iii) Issue of spirit from the spirit store for manufacture : After getting the requirement for manufacture the spirit is then be issued to the manufacturer by the officer incharge. The manufacturers must keep ready all other ingredients of preparation with which the spirit is to be mixed before handing over his spirit immediately on his issue of in presence of the official incharge. The following particulars should be labelled e.g. sect as name and batch no. of preparation, description and quantity of alcohol, date of removal of preparation and quantity of preparation removed.

(iv) Wastage of spirit in manufacture : In the manufacture of medicinal and toilet preparation, there is a inevitable wastage of alcohol varying from preparation to preparation. Permissible percentage of wastage in the manufacture of a particular preparation is fixed by the central government or state government from time to time. The manufacturer will be liable to pay the duty on the excess wastage along with any penalty prescribed by the excise commissioner.

STORAGE OF FINISHED PREPARATION AND WARE HOUSING OF ALCOHOLIC PREPARATION

The name of the preparation, its batch no., strength, date of storage and actual contents in bulk like should be indicated on label of every container. A licence should be obtained by the persons wishing to establish such a warehouse from the excise commissioner of the state by submitting an application alongwith a fee under the act. Goods can be removed from the warehouse only after payment of duty. Only dutiable goods can be deposited in a licensed warehouse. The method of locking and sealing of a warehouse is to be decided by the Excise Commissioner.

EXEMPTED MEDICINAL PREPARATIONS

The following categories of preparations are exempted from excise duty :

(i) Preparations supplied to hospitals and dispensaries controlled by the Central or the State Government or subsidised by them or charitable hospitals and dispensaries under the management of local bodies.

(ii) Preparations supplied to institution supplying medicare to poor and certified by the Principal Medical Officer of the district.

(iii) In the interest of the trade or the public, the Central Government may exempt any other preparation from the levy of duty if it thinks so.

ISSUE OF ALCOHOLIC PREPARATION FROM BONDED LABORATORIES

An application in the prescribed form with duty paid on it must be presented by the manufactures to the Excise office in case he desires to take out any preparation from the bonded laboratory. Preparation may be issued without payment of duty when issued to bonded ware- house or exported to a place outside India or to institutions authorised to receive duty free preparations. The day to day account should be maintained in proper form by the manufacturers.

MANUFACTURE OUTSIDE BOND LICENCE

To manufacture medicinal and tested preparation without bond a licence is necessary.

The following fees are required to be paid:

(i) Rs. 10.00 : For alcohol consumption of 125 LP litre or less per annum.

(ii) Rs. 25.00 : For an alcohol consumption of more than 125 but less than 500 L.P. litre per annum.

(iii) Rs. 200.00 : For an alcohol consumption of 500 L.P. litres or more .

(iv) Rs. 250.00 : For manufacture of Ayurvedic and Unani preparation containing self generated alcohol or containing alcohol produced by distillation provided. It is more than 2%

NON-BONDED LABORATORY

In each non-bonded manufactory there should be spirit store, a laboratory and a finished goods store. There should be only one entrance and only one door each for the laboratory spirit store and finished goods store. The windows, if any, should be covered with iron bars. To shut off gas and electric connection at the end of the day suitable provisions should be provided.

OBTAINING THE SPIRIT

By sending an indend in duplicate with one copy to the distiller or the warehouse people and the other to the Excise Officer-incharge of warehouse and distillary, the spirit can be obtained from a distillery or a spirit ware house immediately after arrival of the spirit so obtained at the non-bonded manufactory and making entry into proper register, the manufactuerer should transfer it to the respective store.

INSPECTION OF THE NON-BONDED LABORATORY

At least once every month the laboratory shall be inspected by the concerned Excise officer. Any officers of prohibition, Hand Revenue of Medical and Public Health Department may be authorised by the State Govt. for inspection of a non-bonded laboratory. The State Government appoint an officer who in this behalf issues a licence for manufacture outside bond on receiving application offer making suitable enquiries.

MANUFACTURE OF AYURVEDIC, HOMOEOPATHIC AND PATENT AND PROPRIATARY PREPARATION

There are 2 types of Ayurvedic preparation containing alcohols i.e. those.

(i) Containing self generated alcohal like Asavas and Aristas.

(ii) Prepared by distillation or those to which alcohal has been added at any stage of the manufacture.

Ayurvedic peparation containing self generated alcohol are considered to non alcoholic for the purpose of this Act and are considered to be exempted from the performance of excise duty of their alcoholic content does not exceed 2%. A duty of Rs. 52.80 per litre of pure alcohal content is liable to be charged on Ayurvedic preparations either made in bond or without bond by distillation with alcohol added at any stage of their manufacture.

EXPORT OF ALCOHLIC PREPARATIONS

Alcohlic preparations which are exported from India are exempted from the payment of duty they can be exported in the following way.

(i) Under bond (without payment of duty from bonded laboratory).

(ii) Under claim for rebate of duty.

(a) Export under bond : Alcohlic preparations under bond can be exported only by those persons who have a bonded-laboratory or a bonded warehouse. The cases of package is which goods for export should contain the specified particulars under the Act for the dutiable goods with their alcoholic contents in L.P. litres.

The officer incharge should seal each package with this official seal in a way that it cannot be tempered with, without breaking the seal.

(b) Export of Duty Paid Goods : It is carried out under claims for rebate of duty. the packing of the goods is to be done under supervision of the excise officer for ascertainingthealcohalic strengthofgoods. The Excise Officer shall take their samples and send them to the chemical examiner. The officer shall enter the strengths of the preparation on the duplicate copy of the application after receipt of the report from the chemical examiner.

For getting the rebate of duty, the exporter must claim

the rebate from the excise commissioner within one month of the issue of export certificate to him and Excise Commissioner may order the refund of duty if he is satisfied about the validity of the claim.

PROCEDURES FOR CONTROL OF MANUFACTURE

UNDER THE ACT

(i) FOR ENTRY, SEARCH AND SEIZURE

Only Excise Officer of the rank of sub inspector and above are authorised. The officer can break open the doors and remove other obstacles in case of any resistance.

(ii) DETENTION OF PERSON

Any person may be stopped and detained by Excise Officers powered by the State Government.

(iii) DISPOSAL OF SEIZED ARTICLES

The disposal of seized articles according to the provisions of the law should be made speedily.

(iv) DISPOSAL ARRESTED PERSONS

The person arrested under the provisions of Act should be immediately sent to the nearest excise officer empowerd to produce them before a Magistrate or to the officer incharge of the police station where there is no excise officer. The arrested person may be admitted to bail before a Magistrate or in default hand over to the judicial custody by the officer within 24 hours of this arrest.

(v) SUMMONS BY EXCISE OFFICER

Any person can be summoned to give an evidence or produce documents by serving on him a written notice to this effect only by Excise Officer of the rank of sub. inspector or above.

OFFENCES AND PENALTIES UNDER THE ACT

(i) Failure to observe conditions of a licence or to pay duty—

(ii) Convince by owners or occupiers of land for offences under the act :

An owner or occupier of a land who willfully convines at the commission of an offence shall be liable to a punishment with an imprisonment up to 6 months or fine up to Rs 500/- or both.

(iii) MALICIOUS INFORMATIONS : IF A PERSON

Willfully gives false information resulting in a arrest or a search to be made the Act is punishable for 2 years or fine up to Rs. 2000/- or both.

(iv) DISORDERLY KEEPING OF STOCKS AND ACCOUNTS

All accounts of goods should be maintained in the prescribed manner. A fine up to Rs. 2000/- shall be liable on a person making false entries or tearing out pages from stock books.

(v) SALE OF DUTIABLE GOODS IN IMPROPER CONDITIONS

A dealer of dutiable goods shall be liable to a fine extending up to Rs. 1,000/- if he is found is possession of unwrapped or unlabelled goods or whose label or wrapperes torn or tampered with.

(vi) FAILURE OF EXCISE OFFICER TO DO DUTY

An excise officer shall be liable to imprisonment extending up to 3 month or to a fine up to 3 months pay or both if he ceases or refuses to do his duty without obtaining permission to that effects from his superiors or with giving 2 months notice.

(vii) FAILURE TO FURNISH PROOF OF EXPORT WITH IN A SPECIFIED PERIOD : A Fine entending maximum to Rs. 2000.00 is made.

(viii) OFFENCES WITH RESPECT TO WARE HOUSING

An owner of a warehouse of any other person his employment may be liable to a fine extending up to rupees 200/-. If he commits any of the following offences like opens any locks or door in the absence of excise officer or makes any alteration in the ware house or removes goods in the contravention of the rules under the Act.

(ix) OBSTRUCTION TO OFFICERS AND GIVING FALS INFORMATION

A person shall be liable to a fine extending to Rs 5,000/- if he willfully obstruct or offers any resistance or gives any false or misleading information to any Excise officer.

(x) DISCLOSURE OF INFORMATION BY EXCISE OFFICERS

An officer disclosing information in bad faith acquired in course of his duty shall be liable to a fine extending up to rupees 1000/-.

(xi) GENERAL PENALTY

A person shall be punishable with a fine extending up to Rs. 1000/- for break of any of the rules made under the Act. Goods shall be liable to confiscation in whose case break has committed.

(xii) POWER OF ADJUDICATION OF CONFISCATION AND PENALTY

The Excise commissioner may adjudge the penalty and confiscation if a person is liable to penalty or an article is liable to confiscation under the rules.

10

THE MEDICAL TERMINATION OF PREGNANCY ACT

INTRODUCTION

The enactment of Medical Termination Act, 1971, Rules 1975 and Regulation 1971 were introduced in India to check the ever increasing population of the country.

Considering the progress made by medical services and spread of facilities in the entire country and to avoid risks to the expectant mothers' health it was decided to liberalise the law regarding abortion. The following reasons were in mind like.

(i) When the pregnancy occurs due to sex crimes or sex with a lunatic woman;

(ii) When a pregnancy is posing grave risk to the life or physical and mental health of a woman;

(iii) When the likelihood of deformities and some serious problems to the child to be born affecting the mothers' health also.

DEFINITIONS

1. Guardian : Means the persons having the care of a minor or a lunatic.

2. Lunatic : It has the meaning assigned to it in section 3 of the Indian Lunacy Act.

3. Minoe : It means a person who is not deemed to have attained majority under the provisions of the Indian Majority Act.

4. Registered Medical Practitioner : Means a person possessing any recognised medical qualification as defined under Indian Medical Council Act and whose name has been entered in a State Medical Register and who has such experience or training in gynaecology and obstetrics as may be prescribed by the rules made under the Act.

5. Admission register : It means a register maintained under regulation 5.

6. Approved place : Means a place approved under rule 4 of the Medical Termination Pregnancy Rules, 1975.

7. Place : Any building, tent, or establishment, hospital, clinic etc., used or intended to be used for the termination of any pregnancies.

OBJECTIONS OF THE ACT

The Medical Termination of Pregnancy Act, 1971 provides for termination of pregnancy only by registered medical practitioner or hospitals established and run by the Central or State Government.

TERMINATION OF PREGNANCIES

The Act provides for the termination of a pregnancy by a registered medical practitioner as follows :

(i) When the length of pregnancy is less than 12 weeks;

(ii) When the length of pregnancy exceeds 12 weeks but does not exceed 20 weeks the opinion of two registered medical practitioners is sought that the—

(a) the continuation of the pregnancy would have a

serious risk to the pregnant woman alongwith a grave injury to her physical or mental health, or

(b) there is a grave risk to the child to be born with certain abnormalities or seriously handicapped.

The provision relating to the opinion of two RMPs shall not apply in case the termination of pregnancy becomes absolutely necessary to save the life of a pregnant woman whose pregnancy exceeds 12 weeks.

Where a pregnancy is caused to a woman by rape, the enxiety caused by such pregnancy shall be presumed to constitute grave injury to the mental health of a pregnant woman.

Any pregnancy occuring on account of a failure of any method used by any married woman or her husband for the purpose of limiting the number of children, the anxiety caused by such unwanted pregnancy may be presumed to constitute a grave injury to the mental well being of the pregnant woman.

No pregnancy shall be terminated without the consent of the pregnant woman except when (a) pregnant woman is less than 18 years in age, or (b) the pregnant woman is a lunatic although she has attained the age of 18 years. Such consent shall be given in Form C.

Termination of pregnancy by a person other than a RMP is an offence punishable under the Indian Penal Code.

Termination of pregnancy shall not be made at any place other than (a) hospital established and run by Government or (b) a place approved for this purpose of this Act by the Government.

Every RMP who terminates any pregnancy should certify the termination in the prescribed Form 1 within three hours of the termination of the pregnancy.

No suit or legal action shall be taken against any RMP for any damage caused or likely to be caused by anything which is done in good faith under this Act.

The RMP should possess one or more of the following experience or training in gynaecology and obsterics :

(i) Whether he was registered in a State Medical Register immediately before the enactment of the Act, experience in the practice of gynaecology and obstetrics for not less than three years.

(ii) An RMP who was registered in a State Medical Register on or after the date of commencement of the Act.

(a) If he has completed six months of house surgery in gynaecology and obstetrics; or

(b) without doing any house surgery he should have experience at some hospital for not less than one year in the practice of gynaecology and obstetrics; or

(c) he should have assisted an RMP in performing of twenty-five cases of medical termination of pregnancy in a hospital established or run, or a training institute approved for this purpose, by the Government.

The Chief Medical Officer of the District shall verify or inspect the place to ascertain himself that proper facilities and conditions are maintained for Medical Termination of Pregnancy.

The Government may approve the place after recommendations of the Chief Medical Officer of the District. The approval certificate must be displayed at a prominent place so that it may be visible to the persons visiting the places.

The Chief Medical Officer of the District may inspect an approved place whenever he desires. If he is not satisfied with the facilities or proper conditions, hygienic or otherwise, he shall report this to the authorities. On receipt of such report the Government may give reasonable time to the owner for being heard either cancel the certificate of approval or suspend the same for such a period as it may think fit. The certificate may be renewed after making required improvements.

Every head of the hospital or owner of the approved place shall maintain a register to record therein the admissions of women for termination of pregnancies. The register shall be a secret document. The entries will be serially and yearwise e.g. 5/93 refers to serial No. 5 of 1993.

The admission register shall not be open to anybody for inspection except under the authority of :

(i) In case of a departmental or other enquiry, the Chief Secretary to the Government of a Union Territory;

(ii) In the case of an investigation into an offence;

(iii) In the case of a suit or other action for damages.

11

THE CONSEQUENCES OF PHARMACEUTICAL PATENT PROTECTION

INTRODUCTION

Pharmaceutical Patents: Their Purpose And Limitations

Patents are intended to stimulate invention by protecting original results for a specified period of exclusivity durig which the inventor may use or voluntarily license others to use, the invention without competition from copiers.

* Product patents cover new composition of matter with demonstrable utility
* Process patents protect novel methos of production of new or known substances
* Use patents apply to newly invented uses of a new or known substances

For the pharmaceuticals, product patents are the tightest form of protection and potentially the most rewarding for the patentee. Process patents are generally far less effective, because they can often be circumvented by the substitution of minor process variants.

The overriding purpose of patents is to promote the development of innovative drug therapy. here will be virtually no development of therapetutically innovative new deugs without adequate patent protection. Applying the strictest test for quality and acceptance, out of 775 new drug substances introduced between 1975-89, only 66 new drugs were both therapeutically innovative and globally marketed: all but two of these drugs were discovered in countries where strong patent protection already existed at the beginning of the period studied (i.e. 1975).

NEW HORIZONS IN INDIA

1. BATTLE OF PRINCIPLES 1970-'93

The past quarter of a century has witnessed a 'Battle of Principles' over pharmaceutical patent protection in India. The Indian government and the local pharmaceutical industry have unheld the principle of giving only very limited patent protection for drugs as being in the national interest.

The research based multinational pharmaceutical industry, on the other hand, regarded Indian patent protection as totally inadequate. The recongnition of strong patent protection is, in their view, a pre-condition for investment by a research based industry.

(i) Indian Patents Act

The Patents Act 1970 (imlemented on 20th April, 1972) was not an accidental piece of legislation but a deliberate assertion of the national will.

* No pharmaceutical product patents, only process patents are admissible
* The Indian patent term of 14 years from the date of filing is, for pharmaceutical processes, curtailed to 7 years from the date of filing or 5 years from the date of sealing patent, which ever is the shorter
* Pharmaceutical process patents are automatically deemed to be endorsed Licence of Right 3 years from the date of sealing a pharmaceutical patent.

Under such Licence of Right, a maximum royalty of 4% of the net ex-works bulk selling price of the drug made by the patented process is payable by the licensee.

In addition, pharmaceutical patents are subject to compulsory licensing at the direction of the Controller of patents, 3 years from the date or sealing a patent "on the ground that the reasonable requirements of the public with respect to the patented invention have not been satisfied, or that the patented product is not available to the public at a reasonable price". Patents must be 'worked' within 3 years of the date of sealing. This requirements involves manufacturing in India on a commercial scale. In addition, the Indian government may use, or authorise others to use on its behalf, any patented invention.

This act, which is still in force, does not permit patent cover for pharmaceutical products. Processes are patentable, but only for a period that is so short that most such patents will have expired before the releant drug is ready for market introduction. In reality, there is no effective pharmaceutical patent protection in India.

(ii) The Rise of the Indian Pharmaceutical Industry and the Decling of Multinationals

By abolishing product patents, the Patent Act 1970 has made it legally permissible in India for anyone with adequate chemical skills to 'copy' the active ingredients of drugs which are patent protected in countries that provide product cover.

The extremely short period of patent cover has persuaded most foreign research based drug companies that it is not worthwhile to go to the trouble of applying for process patents in the first place. Even if there is no opposition, it takes atleast 6 years before a patent is issued and it could stretch to 8-10 years if an opposition is filed. Since this period bites into the duration of the patent, it becomes a complete farce in the case of pharma and other patents, where the duration is 7 years from the date of filing of the patent or 5 years from the date of sealing whichever is less. MNCs in India usually doesn't apply for patents because, the patent cover is so inadequate that it does not justify the cost, effort or disclosures involved in seeking protection. Even after obtaining patent, the onus of proving infringment is on the patentee.

In short, the Patents Act 1970 doesn't in reality protct pharmaceutical processes.

The virtual abolition of pharmaceutical patent protection was the spring board that enabled Indian Pharmaceutical companies, from a modest position in 1970, to 'conquer' more than three-fifths of the Indian pharmacy market by 1993.

During the period of 1970-93, the recorded trend in facour of local industry from as little as 10-20% to over 60% of the market in just over twodecades is probaly unparalleled in world markets, as it the multinational loss of 11% points of market shae in little more thandecade (1982-93) (Chart 1). Elsewhere in the world, the tendency over the same period has generally been the world, the tendency over the same period has generally been the reverse; the foreign market share has risen at the expense of locally owned industry as the drug market overall has 'globalised'.

India's possession of chemical infrastructure and process skills; the competitive determination of Indian companies; and the decision by many MNCs to downgrade oreven 'writer off' India in their global investment and marketing strategy, were ultimately decisive. The effective elimination of patent protection was a major enabling factor.

The ownership and investment restrictions under FERA, severe drug price control, thefear of establishing low price precedents for patented drugs leading to 'leaage' into higher priced markets and unwillingness to provide proprieary clinical and biomedical information to a country that was not prepared to respect intellectual property rights for pharmaceuticals are the other rasons why MNCs restricted their operation in India.

The net results can be observed by comparing the world raning (by sales value) of leading multinationals with their ran in India. Only 2 of the world's Top-Ten pharmaceutical groups are also in the Top-Ten in India; similarly, 6 of the world's Top-Twenty and 10 of the Top-Thirty are in the corresponding Indian raning group.

Another wayof looking at the situation is to consider how many of the world's Top-Thirty have direct investments in pharmaceutical companies in Indian (Chart 2).

It can be seen that only just over half of the world's Top-Thirty pharmaceutical groups have a dierect investment in India. European companies have generally retained their direct presence in India, though most have been obliged to reduce their ownership to or below 40%. Only one of the eleven European groups in the world's Top-Thirty has so far opted out, but most have been cautious about adding to their investment in India under the prevailing restrictions.

The US has 14 representatives among the world'sTop-Thirty, but only 6 of these have a direct presence in India. None of the 5. Japanese companies in the world's Top-Thirty are directly active in the Indian market.

The consequential but long-delayed counter-action by multinational companies to recover their patent rights in India through the 'TRIPS' Agreement under GATT is neither wicked, nor 'colonial', nor in any way surprising. The impassioned confrontation between Indian and multinational companies over the 'Dunkel Draft' that led to the 'TRIPS' Agreement under GATT should be seen in this light.

(iii) 'Trips' and the Dispute Over Pharmaceutical Patent Protection

Collectively, the Indian pharmaceutical industry is of the view that the existing system which permits the early copying of drugs that are patent protected elsewhere, is one that promotes competition by nipping monopoly in the bud.

Conversely, the research-based multinational drug industry considers that the denial of patent rights operates as a protectionist measure, shielding Indian companies from real pharmaceutical competition: that of the innovator. According to this view, the 'free ride' on intellectual property created by others is not a form of competition but one of expropriation.

The clash of principles as well as self-interet represented by those opposing views is at the heart of the dispute over 'RIPS'.

TRIPS Agreement covers patents, trademarks, copyright, industrial designs and other forms of intellectual property. Only patents will be discussed in this study.

The inssertion of intellectual property into the negotiations occurred at the very outset, in Punta del Este, Uruguay, in September 1986. The USA insisted on placing "services, intellectual property, and foreign investment restrictions on agenda despite objections from developing countries led by India and Brazil".

It was hardly surprising that the inclusion of services and intellectual property were a major objective of the US and industrialised countries generally. Services represent 70% of US GDP and around 60% of most West European countries and Japan.

The main thrust of the Dunkel Draft, in so far as it applies TRIPS to pharmaceuticals, was:

* to provide a minimum patent term of 20 years from the date of filing
* to end exclusion of pharmaceutical products from patent protection
* to accept importation as 'working' a patent
* to restrict compulosry licensing to particular circumstances rather than allowing its use as a weapon of discrimination for the furtherance of national objectives
* to reverse the burden of proof ininfringement actions relating to process patents
* to provide transitional arrangements, deferring the acceptance of pharmaceutical product patents by developing countries of ten years.

to deny retrospective protection for existing products, but to grant limited exclusivity in developing countries for pharmaceutical products whose patent applications are filed after the TRIPS Agreement comes into force.

The first five items are basically in line with the requirements of the industrialised world, where as the last two-especially the 6th–are concessions to the demands of developing countries.

The government of India was publicy defending Dunkel as being basically compatible with India's interests, though certain changes in the TRIPS provisions were desired. The opponents of pharmaceutical patent protection, however, had defined their mninmum aims for the renegotiation of TRIPS:

* Importation not betreated as 'working' a patent
* Retention of compulsory licensing as under The Patents Act 1970
* Retention of automatic licences of right as before
* No reversal of the burden of proof in process patent litigation

As the negotiations entered their final phase, opposition to TRIPS onthe part of the Indian pharmaceutical industry, as represented by IDMA, rose to a climax at their International Conference on Patent Regime Proposed in the Uruguay Round, held inNew Delhi in September 1993, where apocaloyptic warnings were sounded by I.A. Modi:

* price of drugs shall go high by 5 to 20 times
* supply in the market will be affected as it will depend on imports
* national drug industry will not be developed and it will not be able to generate fresh investment from internal sources
* export will be affected
* indigenous R&D efforts will die and permanent dependence on imported technologies will be created

Contrary views were expressed in a position paper by the Inerpat-India Task Force:

"If we strengthen our patent law, new opportunities for export will unfold before us. In the field of drugs, we have technological capabilities. We have a reservoir of scientific and technical man power, whose cost in terms of salaries and wages is one third of that in Japan and one fifth that of US. We have the potential to become a cost effective producer of drugs. Once the crutches of weak patent law are removed, we can successfully negotiate with reserch-based multinational companies, which undertake contract manufacture of sophisticated new drugs and intermediate chemicals in bulk for buy back and export earnings, create more employment, help fuller utilisation of capacities and also result in transfer of technology and knowhow".

On December 15, 1993, India initialled the Draft Final Act of Uruguay Round, including the Agreement, on Trade-Related Intellectual Property Rights.

Let no one imagine that the conflict over pharmaceutical patent protection in India is over.

Yet, in the unpredictable world of pharmapolitics, one conclusion can be drawn with certainty: there will be profound change. The TRIPS Agreement will open new horizons in India for everyone in the pharmaceutical industry.

2. THE CONSEQUENCES OF 'TRIPS'-FACTS, MYTHS AND PROSPECTS

The 'Agreement on Trade-Related Aspects of Intellectual Property Rights, including trade in counterfeit goods', being part of the Draft Final Act of the Uruguay Round, is expected to be ratified by participating countries during the course of 1994 and come into force in 1995.

The real and decisive battle will not, however, be fought over ratification but later, over interpretation, implementation and enforcement.

(i) Pharmaceutical Patents Under 'Trips'

The salient features of the Agreement on 'TRIPS' as it affects pharmaceutical patent are:

Article 27-Patentable Subject Matter: Product patents are to be available "in all fields of technology" and patent rights "enjoyable without discrimination. whetehr products are imported or locally produced". In other words, importation is to be recognised as 'working' a patent.

Article 28-Right Conferred: Patents are to confer exclusive rights preventing third parties from copying the patented product, process or product obtained directly by the process, without the owner's consent.

Article 30-Exception to Rights Conferred: Verbatim: "Memberes may provide limited exceptions to the exclusive rights conferred by the patent, provided that such exceptions do not unreasonably conflict with a normal exploitation of the patent and do not confilict with a normal exploitation of the patent and do not unreasonably prejudice the legitimate interests of the patent owner, taking account of the legitimate interests of third parties".

Article 31-Other Use Without Autorization of the Right Holder: This article specifies how national legislation permitting, for example compulsory licensing or licences of ritht ("including use by the government or third parties authorized by the government"), are to be applied whilst respecting certain limiting provisions which are set out in 12 sub-clauses.

In the context of this Study, the most important of these provisions are:

31 (b): The aspiring licensee must "have made efforts to obtain authorization from the right holder on reasonable commercial terms and conditions" and have failed to obtain it "within a reasonable period of time". This requirement may, however, be waived "in the case of a national emergency or other circumstances of extreme urgency or in cases of public non commercial use".

31 (f): "any such use shall be authorized predominantly for the supply of the domestic market."

31 (h): "the right holder shall be paid adequate remuneration in the circimstances of each case, taking into account the economic value of the authorization".

31 (k): The conditions under (b) and (f) are not obligatory where "such use is permitted to remedy a practice dtermined after judicial or administrative process to be anti-competitive".

Article 33-term of Protection: his "shall not end before the expiration of a period of twenty years counted from the filing date".

Article 34-Process Patents: Burden of Proof: This reverses the burden of proof, ordering "the defendant to prove that the process to obtain an identical product is different from the patented process".

Article 41-Enforcement-General Obligations: This requires the signatories to "ensure that enforcement procedures. are available under their national laws".

Article 65-67-Transtitional Arrangement: Generally, the provisions of the 'TRIPS' Agreement are to be applied within "one year following thedate of entry into force of the Agreement Establishing the WTO but entitlement todelay is granted to developing countries and to those undergoing transformation from a centrally-planned into a market economy.

Article 70-Protection for Existing Subject Matter: "There shall be no obligation torestore protection to subject matter which on the date of application of this Agreement for the Member in question has fallen into the public domain". It means that neither existing products nor pipeline drugs with published patents can be protected in India. However, 70/8 and 70/9 provide the so-called 'Black Box' arrangements for new pharmaceutical inventions in countries like India when 'TRIPS' comes into force. Under these provisions, a means of filing patent appliations must be provided by countries like India, allowing the claimed priority date and a full term of protection. For products qualifying for such treatment, "exclusive marketing rights shall be granted for a period of five years after obtaining marketing approval or until a product patent is granted or rejected whichever period is shorter".

The above summary implies that, subject to its ratification, the 'TRIPS' Agreement will oblige India to bring its patent legislation into line with normal practice in the industrialise countries.

The transitional period of 10 years means, however, that pharmaceutical product patent-which are generally regarded as essential to give real and adequate protection-during the allotted term-will not have to be adopted by India until the year 200. That date is based on the assumption that the agreement setting up WTO comes into force in 1995.

Management of Indian companies will therefore have a decade to prepare for a new era, while management of MNCs will have to wait throughout that decade for real pharmaceutical patent protection. This will no doubt test Indian adaptability and mltinational patience to the limit.

(ii) On the Threshold of a New Era

The reactions to 'TRIPS' were favourable in Europe Washingtion was in two minds, welcoming most of the Agreement but deploring the length of the transtitional period and comtemplating renewed pressure in bilateral negotiations to remedy this. Reception in India was divided between enthusiastic applause, philosophical resignation and furious resentment.

Whether the forward look will now prevail over the backward glance remains to be seen. The dynamics of a new era can work both ways: they can promote or obstruct change and the opportunities for obstruction are by no means negligible.

Even before the TRIPS accord was concluded, a panel of tetired judges was et up by India's National Working Group on Patent Laws, to examine the constitutional aspects of the proposals. This was followed by petitions to the Supreme Court challenging the constitutional validity of the "TRIPS" agreement.

In practical term it is, however, the events after the presumed ratification of "TRIPS" that will determine whether static or dynamic policies will set the one for India under a new patent regime.

(iii) The Speed and Depth of Patent Penetration of

India's Drug Market

Myth: India will, as a result of "TRIPS", be overrunby MNCs whose patents will pre-empt most of the pharmaceutical market and more or less 'wipe out" companies.

Fact: Approximately 10% by value of India's drug market would have been patent-protected in 1993, had India been operating under European-style Pharmaceutical patent process

The construction of an Indian market model under 'national' patent protection, as it would have looked in 1993 had European-Style drug patents been operative in India, proves that at least 90% by value of the Indian pharmaceutical market was free from 'notional' patent cover (Chart 3 and 4).

Prospects: Starting ten years from now, patent protection will gradually rise to a level of up to 15% of the market by value. The intervening decade will provide many advantageous opportunities for adaptation to the new patent regime.

(iv) Why Drugs Prices Will Not explode

Myth: Patents under 'TRIPS' will cause an instant and lasting pric explosion on the Indian drug market. MNCs will be at complete liberty to let prices soar.

FACT: Patent protection will have no noticeable impact on prices before 2003 at the earliest, and cannot build up significantly until after 2005.

Prospects: At any one time, not more than 15% of the Indian market is likely to be exposed to patent-based premium pricing. The existence of checks and balances will constrain the pricing of most new drugs under patent. There will be no general price 'explosion'.

More important than the time scale of patent protection will be fundamental 'checks and balances' which will put a brake on the impact of premium pricing on Indian drug expenditure, namely:

* the low purchasing power of Indian patents

* government price control under permanent or reserve powers
* thereapeutic competition from cheaper, unpatented drugs

of these, the second is the most immediate, wherea the first and third are the most durable safeguards agains a price 'explosion'.

Only 4% of the Indian population is covered by Goverr ment and State health insurance. Most of the populatio pay the full cost of drugs out-of-pocket. Average India purchasing power is one-twentieth of that in the USA. Ther is every reason to suppose that the Indian 'out-of-pocket' drug market can, for the foreseable future, be effectively self-regulating in terms of drug ricing, without the need for the government to intervene.

With the limited purchasing power of Indian patients, price differences between therapeutically competitive drug substances play a major role in drug choice by Indian doctors and in drug compliance or non-compliance for financial reasons by patients.

A case study of premium-priced quinolone antibacterials-which are not price controlled in India-between 1990 and 1993 demonstrates the contrast between 'high price-high sales value-low volume' of more expensive ciproflozacin and the 'medium price-high volume' sales of cheaper norflozacin, despite the more limited clinical indications for the latter (Chart 5).

Analysis of the bumber of prescriptions shows norflozacin with double the prescription volume of ciprofloxacin but only half the sale value (Chart 5). Nor have the quinolones ousted the much cheaper, older antibiotics as some observers have alleged.

(v) The Outlook for Pharmaceutical Research and Development in India

The main pre-conditions for innovative pharmaceutical R&D are:

* scientific infrastructure

* watertight patent protection for an adequate time period
* good profitability

India lacks both the second and third prerequisites, but patent protection is 'on th eay'.

Lack of patent cover and low profitability are mainly responsible for the fact that the pharmaceutical industry in India's private sector spends only 1.5% of sales on R&D, with Indian companies spending slightly more than the MNCs in India. By comparison, the parent groups of the MNCs in the Indian sample group spent an unweighted average of 15.8% of their global pharmaceutical sales on R&D.

For Indian companies, scale factors inherent in R&D operations are problematic, but not insuperable. In the first place the low cost of scientific staff (responsible for about 3/4 of R&D expenditure in the industrialised countries) represents a distinct and major cost advantage. Secondly, the full cost of R&D can be segmented by concentrating initially on 'R' and collaborating on 'D' outside India with foreign companies. Cost sharing, contracting out, or licensing are all ralistic possibilities for a patentable invention, and that can include the cost of foreign patenting, either shared or as a form of 'advance royalties'.

The Case of Japan, 1960-1992' is analysed, showing that the position there of pharmaceutical patents and R&D up to the mid-1970s resembles India's today in many respects. The 'copying culture' of the Japanese pharmaceutical industry was transformed in the run-up to product patents which, after a similar debate to that in India today, were first granted in 1976.

A 'Before and After' analysis of the innovative record of Japanese pharmaceutical companies in terms of their development of 'Major Global Drugs' is illuminating (Chart 6 and 7).

The subsequent switch of emphasis in Japan towards innovative R&D has produced very good results, both in terms of major innovation and in a crop of patentable drugs which, whilst not the first in the filed, have been good enough to achieve worldwide medical and commercial acceptance-mostly under licence or in joint development projects with multinational companies.

The 'Japanese Case' is sufficiently indicative to prompt the question: if in Japan, why not in India? Indeed, several leaders of the Indian-owned pharmaceutical industry have already committed themselves to such a course.

(vi) Profit and Industrial Strategy

A 'virtuous circle', leading from pharmaceutical patent protection via investment in R&d in India to indusrial expansion requires profit. Risks are much higher than in 'copying'. Profitability, too, must be higher so as to enable industry to take up a commensurate risk posture.

A sample of 15 companies (all in India's pharma Top-30) produced 1992/93 pre-tak profit averaging 5.9% of sales for Indian companies and 5.5% for the subsidiaries of MNCs. It is worth noting that, in India, non-pharmaceutical activities and exports are nore profitable than drug sales on the domestic market on which the greatest part of total sales of these companies is dependent (Chart 8).

By comparison, the multinational parent companies in the same sample achieved pre-tax profits of 18.4% of their global pharmaceutical sales in 1991/92.

The financial 'pool' from which R&D funds are drawn is, in essence, the sum of pre-tax profit and R&D expenditure: it may be termed 'Available Revenue' for R&D. Comparison of this between Indian and foreign companies shows dramatic differences (Chart 9).

For India, it is suggested that 'Available Revenue' would have to rise from the existing 7% at least to 15-18% of sales inorder to back sustainable R&D with adequate financial resources and a minimum cushion of profit.

The existing price control system in India forcibly erodes profit margins by inflexibility and delay. Its early relaxation, along the lines indicated, would be a prerequisite for widespread adoption of a research-based strategy by indigenous and multinational drug companies in India.

3. AT THE CROSS ROADS

1. In Transit

The behavioural pattern of opposing groups during the transitional period leading to full patent protection under 'TRIPS' will determine whether the outcome is to be negative or constructive.

With mischievous intent. Indian drug companies, Government, and MNCs could each try to undermine the Agreement. Methods of doing so could range from the obstructive interpretation of ambiguities in its text to the imposition of ground rules that would prevent the recorientation of a 'copying' culture towards Innovation, were this to happen, a histroic change would have been missed.

The outcome is nnot predicable, but options that will shaps the 'end game' can be examined.

2. Options and End Game

Indian pharmaceutical companies face dificult choices but have to adapt because patent protection will come. Adaptation can be graded: first building on strength to acquire world stature in generic bulk drugs; second, collaborating in India with foreign companies in licensing, co-marketing, or joint ventures for patented drugs; third building up their own research and development in order ultimately to benefit directly from patent protection. A positive follow on strategy would not only involive patent protection but changes in the ground rules that can help to lift the Indian drug industry out of its 'copying' mode and at the same time encourage multinationals to invest in India. The main additional inventive would be a sufficient relaxation of drug price control to underpin investment risk with good financial returns.

MNCs are not obliged to operate in India, but would be short-sighted to cast aside a large, fast-growing, high volume pharmaceutical market because of past and present problems with patents, pricing, ownership and other constraints. Wait and see, is a preferable and more realistic option.

Multinatioanls would also need to adaapt their development policies to India's needs and susceptibilities-as India perceives them.

There is in the first place, the overriding problem of how to fit low Indian prices-conditioned by low Indian purchasing power-into a theoretically desirable but in practice unmanageable policy of 'global' pricing. This difficulty would not disappear even under pricing freedom in India, although a nore flexible pricing system would help to alleviate it.

Other questions of adaptation are collaboration between multinationals and Indian companies in co-marketing patented drugs and other joint ventures, as well as a degree multinational willingness to contemplate investment in local manufacturing where this is economically justifiabe.

The most committed and advanced option for multinational is innovative R&D in India. This pre-suppose full patent protection and improved ground rules for drug pricing and corporate ownership.

The course of the 'end game' is not predictable today. It will depend upon how the 'players' decide to interact. A 'soft landing' can occur if moderate opinion leaders on all sides are prepared to fashion a constructive consensus. This would be a strong signal for industry to select forward-strategic options, for it would prove that Government and both sides of industry had decisively broken with outdated concepts and were ready to move towards New Horizons in India.

Chart 1

INDIAN PHARMACY MARKET 1970-1993

% SHARE BY CORPORATE OWNERSHIP

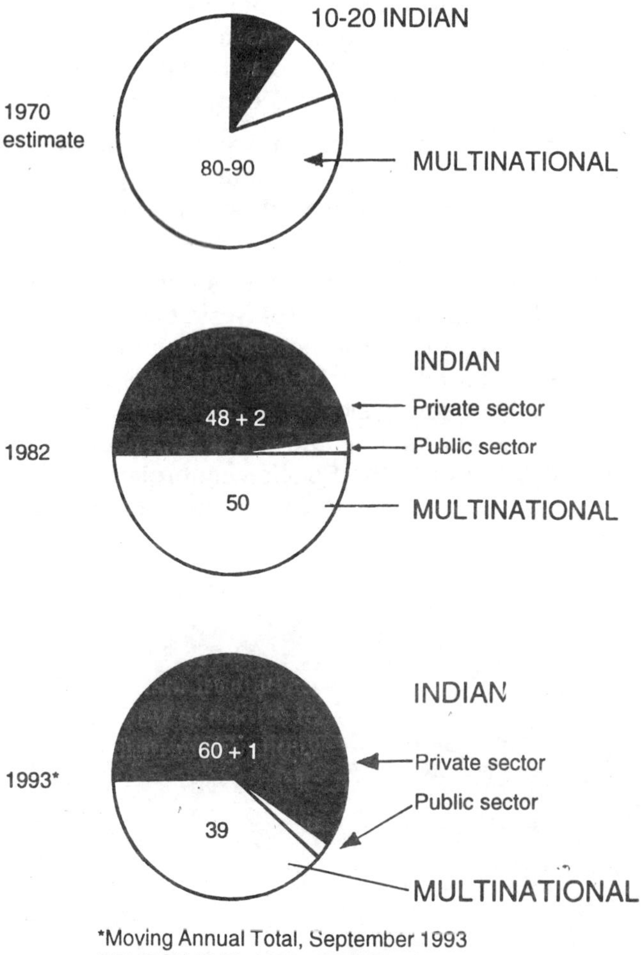

*Moving Annual Total, September 1993
SOURCE 1982, 1993 : ORG Bombay

Chart 2

DIRECT PHARMACEUTICAL INVESTMENT IN INDIA, end-1993 BY WORLD'S TOP-THIRTY DRUG COMPANIES

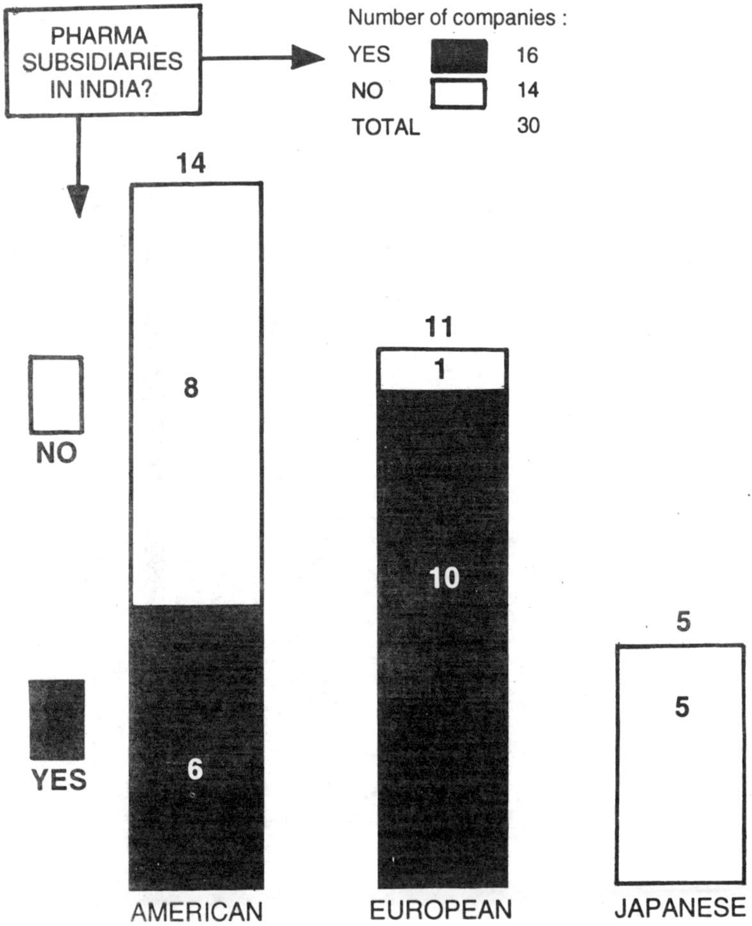

SOURCES : 'World' — Scrip's Pharmaceutical Company League Tables 1992
'India' — ORG Bombay 1993

Chart 3

PATENT EXPIRY MODEL—INDIA 1994-2001 PROSPECTIVE

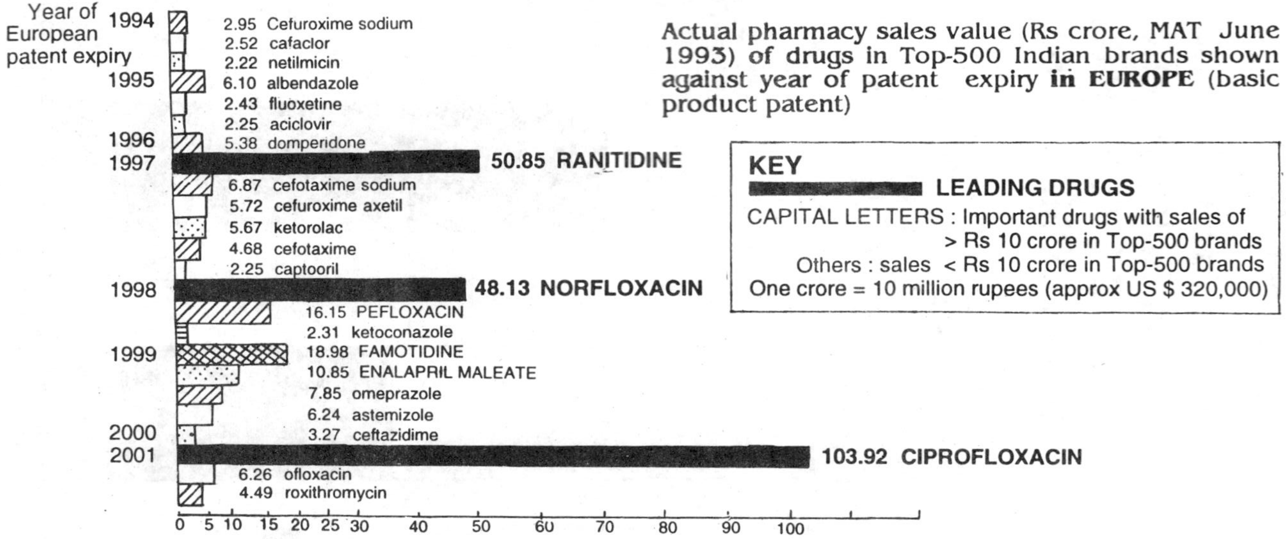

INDIAN SALES IN TOP-500 BRANDS, MAT JUNE 1993 (Rs crore)

SOURCE : ORG BOMBAY, PHARMACY AUDIT, JUNE 1993

Chart 4

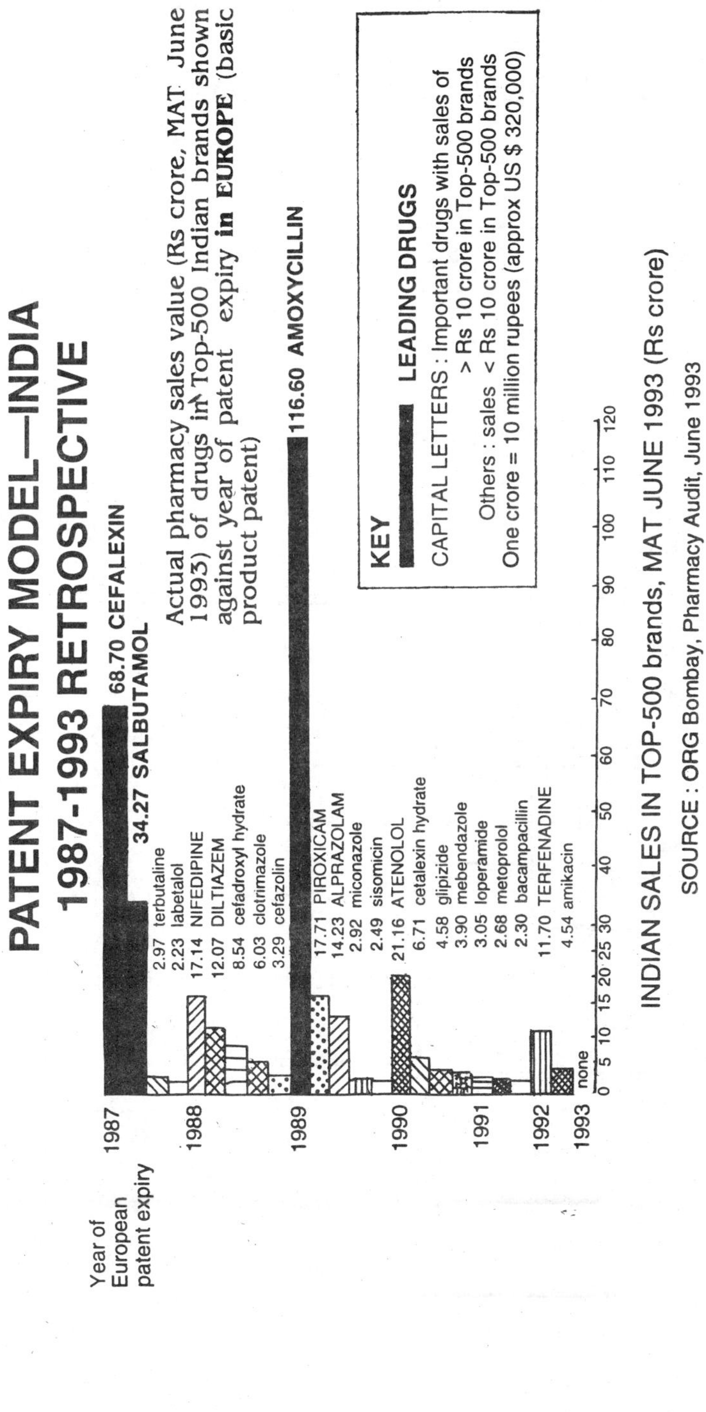
PATENT EXPIRY MODEL—INDIA
1987-1993 RETROSPECTIVE
Year of European patent expiry
1987
1988
1989
1990
1991
1992
1993
68.70 CEFALEXIN
34.27 SALBUTAMOL
2.97 terbutaline
2.23 labetalol
17.14 NIFEDIPINE
12.07 DILTIAZEM
8.54 cefadroxyl hydrate
6.03 clotrimazole
3.29 cefazolin
116.60 AMOXYCILLIN
17.71 PIROXICAM
14.23 ALPRAZOLAM
2.92 miconazole
2.49 sisomicin
21.16 ATENOLOL
6.71 cetalexin hydrate
4.58 glipizide
3.90 mebendazole
3.05 loperamide
2.68 metoprolol
2.30 bacampacillin
11.70 TERFENADINE
4.54 amikacin
none
Actual pharmacy sales value (Rs crore, MAT June 1993) of drugs in Top-500 Indian brands shown against year of patent expiry in EUROPE (basic product patent)
KEY
LEADING DRUGS
CAPITAL LETTERS : Important drugs with sales of > Rs 10 crore in Top-500 brands
Others : sales < Rs 10 crore in Top-500 brands
One crore = 10 million rupees (approx US $ 320,000)
0 5 10 15 20 25 30 40 50 60 70 80 90 100 110 120
INDIAN SALES IN TOP-500 brands, MAT JUNE 1993 (Rs crore)
SOURCE : ORG Bombay, Pharmacy Audit, June 1993

Chart 5

QUINOLONE CASE STUDY, INDIA 1990-1993

VALUE AND VOLUME RATIOS OF NORFLOXACIN : CIPROFLOXACIN

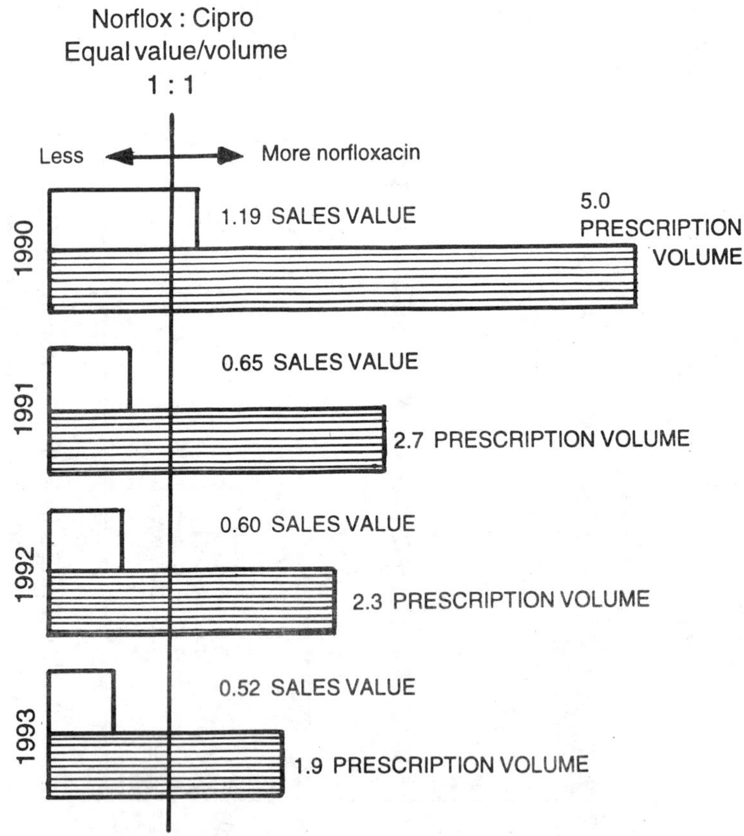

Sales Value : annual
Prescription Volume : March-June each year

SOURCES : Sales Value—study based on ORG data, Bombay
Number of Prescriptions—Cmarc, Calcutta

Chart 6

JAPAN

BEFORE AND AFTER PHARMA PRODUCT PATENTS R&D AND PROFIT, % of SALES 1975, 1990

of 15 major pharmaceutical companies

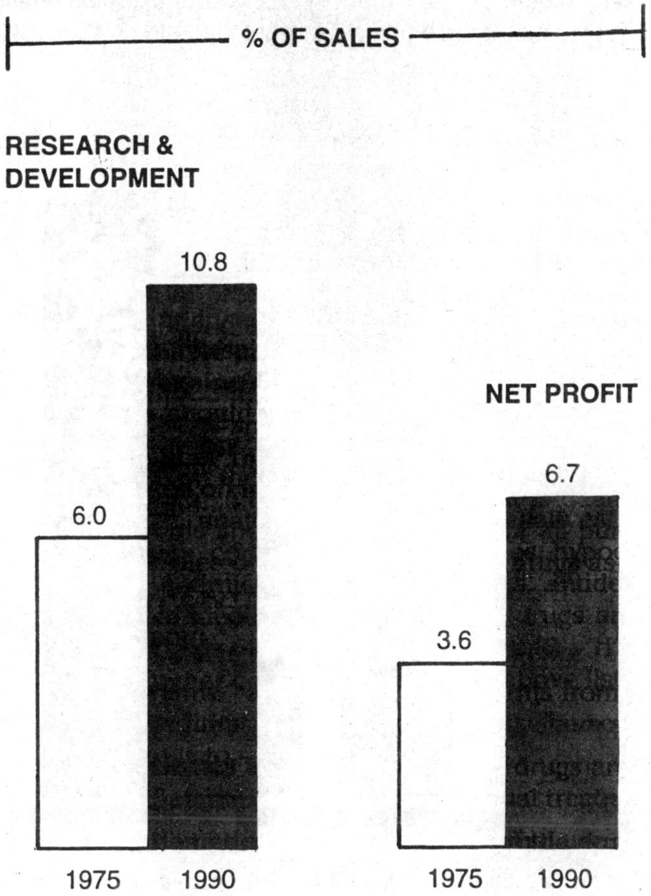

SOURCE: JPMA Guide 1988/89 and 1992 editions

Chart 7

JAPAN

BEFORE AND AFTER PHARMA PRODUCT PATENTS

% share of worldwide origination of 'MAJOR GLOBAL DRUGS' 1960—May 1992

Drug product patents accepted from 1976 in Japan
'Major global Drugs' = marketed or 'pre-registration phase' in at least 6 of the world's 7 largest markets by May 1992

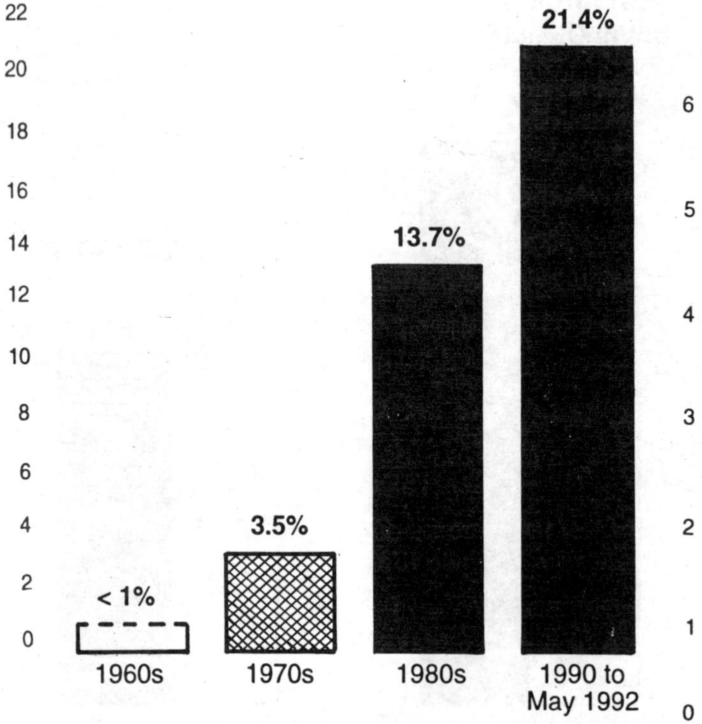

SOURCE: Redwood, "Price Regulation & Pharmaceutical Research" 1993 and supplementary data from Japan

Chart 8

PHARMA PROFIT TREND

INDIA 1988-89 to 1992-1993

OPPI Membership Surveys:

1992-93: 32 Pharmaceutical companies = 43% of total drug sales
1991-92: 28 Pharmaceutical companies = 41% of total drug sales
1988-89: 32 Pharmaceutical companies = 45% of total drug sales

Pre-tax profit, % of Sales

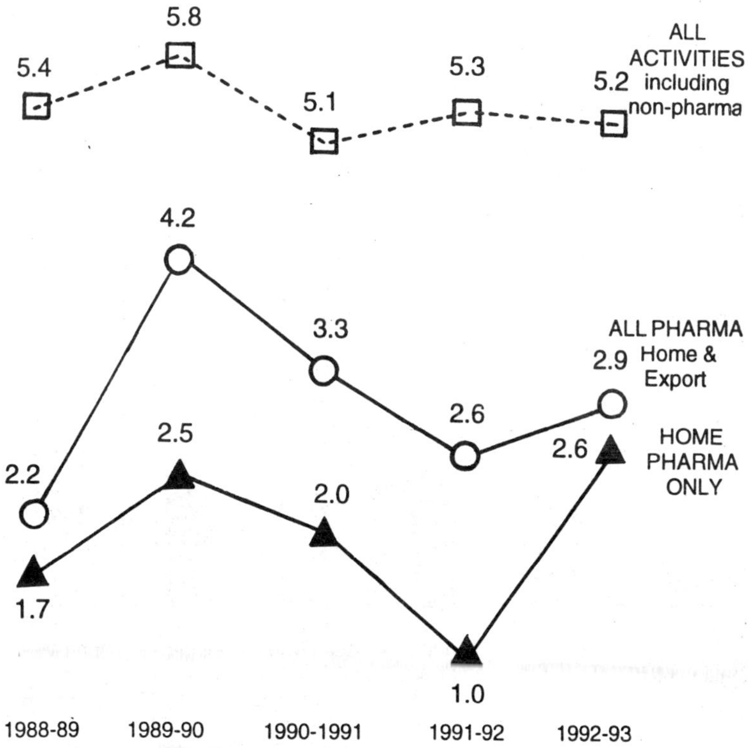

SOURCE: OPPI 27th Annual Report & supplementary data for 1992-93

Chart 9

'AVAILABLE REVENUE' (% of sales) IN THE PHARMA INDUSTRY

INTERNATIONAL COMPARISONS

India: 1992/93
Japan: 1991/92, actual net profit, Pre-tax estimate
MNC: Multinationals.
Parent groups: pharma segment 1991/92

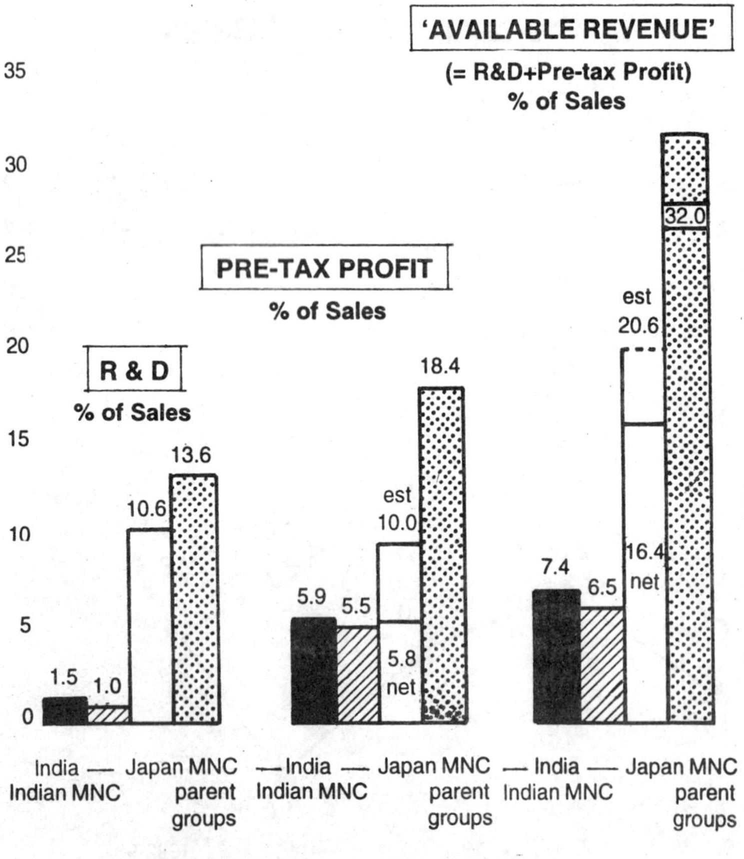

SOURCE: India—Corporate Annual Reports
Others—Scrip's Pharmaceutical Company League Tables 1992

B. Pharma./I—1990 (NS)
Paper III—PHARMACEUTICS-III
(Forensic Pharmacy)

Time : 3 Hours *Maximum Marks :* 80

Attempt any Five *questions.*
All questions carry equal marks.

1. Write down the legal definitions of the following :
   (a) Drug
   (b) Opium
   (c) Retail sale
   (d) Formulation
   (e) Qualified person
   (f) Government Analyst
   (g) Cosmetics
   (h) Trade Commission 2 □□ = 16

2. (a) Describe the duties of Inspectors of premises licensed for sale under the Drugs and Cosmetics Act.
   (b) Discuss the process and condition of cancellation or suspension of a sale licence.
   (c) What are the places through which durg is imported by air into India. 9 + 5 + 2 = 16

3. (a) Explain exempted advertisements.
   (b) Describe the conduct of Pharmacists and their duties in relation to medical profession.
   (c) What are the conditions for the grant of a licence to manufacture for sale of drugs other than those specified in Schedule C and C (1) ?
   3 + 6 + 7 = 16

4. (a) What are the specific labelling requirements for Schedule E, G, H drugs and medicines containing Industrial methylated spirit ?
   (b) Fill in the blanks :
      (i) Indian Pharmacopoeia was first published in............
      (ii) Members of DTAB hold office for...........years.
      (iii) Schedule P prescribes............

(iv) Particulars to be shown in manufacturing record are prescribed in............

(v) Schedule B prescribes............

(vi) The drugs consultative committee meets when required by............ 10 + 6 = 16

5. (a) What is the punishment for stocking and exhibiting for sale various drugs without licence?

(b) Can Central Government prohibit manufacture of any drug and cosmetic in public interest ? Please explain.

(c) Describe the Drugs and Cosmetics (ninth amendment) Rules, 1989. 5 + 5 + 6 = 16

6. (a) What are the conditions for approval of a drug testing laboratory ?

(b) Whether a registered medical practitioner supplying medicines to his own patient needs a licence under the Act or not ? Discuss in brief.

12 + 4 = 16

7. (a) Which drugs and cosmetics are prohibited from manufacture and sale ?

(b) What are the penalties for offences committed under the Poisons Act, 1919 ?

(c) What entitles a person to get registered as a Pharmacist after Education Regulation takes effect in a State ? 6 + 5 + 5 = 16

B. Pharma./I—1991/Supple.
Paper III—PHARMACEUTICS-III
(Forensic Pharmacy)

Time : 3 Hours *Maximum Marks :* 80

Attempt any Five *questions.*
All questions carry equal marks.

1. (i) Define the following :
   (a) Misbranded drugs
   (b) Charas
   (c) Manufactured drugs
   (d) Medicinal preparation.

(ii) What is the punishment for contravention of Sec. 42 of Pharmacy Act ?

(iii) Whether the rules relating to manufacture of drugs are applicable to a Government Institution ?

2. (i) Who issues licence for the import of Schedule O & G drugs.

(ii) What is the qualification prescribed for registration as Pharmacist after implementation of Education Regulations in a State ?

(iii) What is the punishment for allowing the premises to be used for committing an offence under the Dangerous Drugs Act ?

3. (i) Write a brief note on loan licence.

(ii) Fill in the blanks :

(a) The function of CDL for vaccines is carried out at............

(b) The functions of CDL for condoms is carried out at............

(c) The function of CDL for oral poliomyelitis vaccine is carried out at............

(d) Total number of members of a State Pharmacy Council constituted u/s 19 is............

(iii) Who is empowered to sign the certificates of test and analysis under the Drugs and Cosmetics Act and Rules

4. (i) What is the duration of a sale licence ?

(ii) Who issues licences to manufacture for sale drugs under the Drugs and Cosmetics Act and Rules ?

(iii) Which category of drugs are prohibited for import ?

(iv) Who appoints Licensing Authority for sale of drugs?

(v) Can the Licensing Authority delegate his power to sign a licence to his subordinate ?

5. (i) Describe the procedure to be followed by Government Analyst on receipt of sample.

(ii) What are the duties of Inspectors specially authorised to inspect the manufacture of drugs ?

6. (i) Describe the procedure for disposal of confiscated drugs.

(ii) What are the conditions for approval of a Drug

Testing Laboratory ?

7. (i) Name categories of drugs which are prohibited to be manufactured for sale under the Drugs and Cosmetics Act, 1940.

(ii) Define the following :

(a) Adulterated drugs

(b) Cosmetics

(c) Manufacture

(d) Retail sale.

Diploma—1990
PHARMACY—Paper III

[Pharmaceutics III (Forensic Pharmacy and Ethics)]

Time : 3 Hours *Maximum Marks :* 80

Attempt any Five *questions.*
All questions carry equal marks.

1. What are the qualifications specified under Drugs and Cosmetics Rules, 1945 for the Drugs Inspectors ? Discuss briefly their duties for :

(a) inspection of establishments licensed for sale of drugs, and

(b) inspection of establishments licensed for manufacture of drugs.

2. Explain the procedure you would follow in obtaining licence to open a new retail pharmacy shop.
What conditions must be fulfilled before such a licence can be granted ?

3. Define Registered Pharmacist. What are the qualifications required for registration as a Pharmacist under the Pharmacy Act, 1948 ?
When and how is the name of a Registered Pharmacist removed from the State Register ?

4. Define 'Advertisement' and 'Magic Remedies' under the Drugs and Magic Remedies (Objcctionable Advertisements) Act, 1954.

How does advertisement of drugs differ from the advertisement of ordinary goods ?

5. Write short notes on (any *two*) :
   (a) The Poisons Act, 1919
   (b) The Medical Termination of Pregnancy Act, 1971
   (c) The Drugs (Price Control) Order, 1987

6. How does the manufacture of alcoholic preparations 'without bond' differ from that of 'in bond'? Discuss the relative merits and demerits of both.

7. Define the following terms (any *four*) :
   (a) Misbranded drugs
   (b) Repacking of drugs
   (c) Narcotic drug
   (d) New drug
   (e) Homoeopathic tent medicines or proprietary medicines.

Diploma—1991
PHARMACY—Paper III

[Pharmaceutics III (Forensic Pharmacy and Ethics)]

Time : 3 Hours *Maximum Marks :* 80

Attempt any Five *questions.*

1. (a) Define any *two* of the following according to the Drugs & Cosmetics Act, 1940 :
      (i) Misbranded Drugs
      (ii) Adulterated Drugs
      (iii) Spurious Drugs 12
   (b) What is the maximum punishment that can be awarded by courts for offence of sale of such drugs ? 4

2. (a) What are the functions of Central Drugs Laboratory and the Government Analyst ? 8
   (b) What qualifications have been prescribed for appointment of the Government Analyst ? 8

3. How many types of licences can be issued for sale of drugs under Drugs & Cosmetics Act, 1940 and Rules made thereunder. Give a brief account of each of them. 16

4. (a) How are the First and the Subsequent Registers of Pharmacists required to be prepared and maintained under the Pharmacy Act, 1940 ? 8

   (b) What qualifications will entitle a person to have his name registered as a Pharmacist ? 8

5. (a) Define 'Advertisement' and 'Magic Remedies' under the Drugs and Magic Remedies (Objectionable Advertisements) Act, 1954. 8

   (b) What classes of Advertisements are prohibited ? Give examples of each such class. 8

6. (a) What do you understand by the term 'MANUFACTURE IN BOND' as defined in the Medicinal & Toilet Preparations (Excise Duties) Act and Rules ? 8

   (b) What procedure is to be followed in obtaining a licence for the establishment of a bonded laboratory ? 8

7. Write short notes on (Any *Two*) : 16

   (i) Delhi Shops and Establishment Act

   (ii) The Poisons Act, 1919

   (iii) The Medical Termination of Pregnancy Act 1971.

Important Questions from the Chapters

1. Pharmacy Act

(i) Write the constitution and functions of PCI.

(ii) How State Pharmacy Council is constituted under the Act write the functions entruted to it?

(iii) What are Joint State Pharmacy Council. How they are different from State Pharmacy Council give their constitution and functions?

(iv) The Pharmacy Act, 1948, has been enacted to improve the professional standard of Pharmacy in India Explain this fact relating to various provision of the Pharmacy Act.

(v) What do you mean by First and subsequent registers which are required to be prepared and maintained under the Pharmacy Act, 1948?

(vi) Write the qualifications of the persons eligible for being registered as a pharmacist in the Registers and under what circumstances his name can be removed from the registers.

(vii) What is the penalty provided by Act for falsely claiming as a registered pharmacist? How can a person holding a foreign qualification can himself register as a pharmacist?

2. Drugs and Cosmetics Act, 1940

1. Explain the formalities and conditions to be fulfilled for getting a licence for the import of drugs.
2. Write the procedure for obtaining a licence for the manufacture of shedule C and C_1 drugs.
3. What classes of drugs and cosmetics are prohibited to be imported into India.
4. What are loan and repacking licences. what are merits and demerits of loan licence over general licence granted for the manufacture of drugs.
5. Define Adulterated, spurions and misbranded drugs.

Discuss the requirements of building, space and equipment mentioned in schedule M for the manufacture of drugs.

6. Write the qualifications required by a person to become a technical person to carry out the manufacture of various classes of drugs.
7. Explain briefly the terms namely Drug Stores, Chemist and Druggists and Pharmacy. What are the requirements for Pharmacy under the Act.
8. Give the labelling requirements for the following categories of drugs
   - (a) Schedule G drugs
   - (b) Schedule C drugs
   - (c) Schedule X drugs
   - (d) Patent & Proprietary medicines
   - (e) Veterinary drugs
9. What is DTAB and Drugs Consultative Committee. Write their constitution, functions and powers entrusted to them.
10. What are the functions of Central Drugs Laboratory and Government Analysist. Write the qualifications requirements for being a Government Analyst ?

3. Drugs and Magic Remedies (Objectionable Advertisement) Act

1. What are objectionable advertisements under the Drugs and Magic Remedies Act ?
2. Explain breifly the objectives of Drugs and Magic Remedies (objectionable Advertisement Act)

4. Narcotic and Psychotropic substances Act, 1985

1. What operators are prohibited under Narcotic Drugs and Psychotropic Substances Act, 1988 ?
2. "Drug Addiction is a current problem for developing and developed countries." How the Narcotic Drugs and Psychotropic Substances Act is useful in handling the problem said.

3. Define coca leaf, prepared opium, medicinal opium and manufactured Drugs. How the Act is lawful for the manufacture of Prepared Opium by a firm licenced to manufacture "Manufactured Drugs" ?
4. Write briefly the conditions to be satisfied for the cultivation of poppy plant under the Act.
5. Explain the rules relating to the export, import and transshipment of narcotic drugs. What are offences and penalties under the Narcotic Drugs and Psychotropic Substances Act.
6. What is the procedure required to the followed for the disposal of articles and persons arrested and seized under the Act.
7. Explain breifly
   (i) Operators related to Narcotic and Psychotropic Substances that make 'illicit traffic'
   (ii) What officers are authorised to detain persons to prevent them from 'illicit traffic' in the Act.

5. Latest Drugs (Price Control) Order in force

1. What are category I and category II formulations. Discuss the provisions relating to the revision of prices of the formulations under the Act ?
2. How the prices of drugs in bulk and of the drug formulation are calculated under the drug price control order.
3. What are the main provisions of the Drug (price control) order-1979 ? How the retail price of formulations is calculated.
4. Explain the following terms with examples
   (a) Drug prices equalisation Account.
   (b) Retail prices of formulations.
   (c) Price of Bulk Drugs.
5. Discuss the provisions relating to revision of prices of formulations. What are the category I, II and III formulations ?

6. **Poison Act**

   1. Write the restrictions under the Act on the import, possession and sale of poisons in India.

   2. Write briefly the provisions mentioned under the Poison Act, 1919.

7. **Medicinal and Toilet Preparations (Excise Duties) Act, 1955**

   1. Write briefly the procedure for obtaining a licence for a Bonded Laboratory.

   2. How alcoholic preparations are issued from a bonded laboratory and what classes of preparations can be issued duty free ?

   3. What conditions are to be fulfilled by the laboratory meant for the manufacture of alcoholic preparations?

   4. Explain the rules relating to manufacture of alcoholic, Ayurvedic and Homeopathic preparations under the Medicinal and Toilet Preparations (Excise Duties) Act.

   5. Explain briefly the following terms

      (a) Manufacture in bond

      (b) Warehousing of alcoholic preparations

      (c) Export of alcoholic preparations under the bond

      (d) Manufacture outside the bond

8. **Medical Termination of Pregnancy**

   1. Discuss under what circumstances the termination of pregnancy is legal.

   2. Who are the persons eligible for terminating a pregnancy and under what circumstances ?

   3. Write briefly the provisions under the Medical termination of Pregnancy Act. Can this Act be useful for controlling Population problem in our country.

   4. Write short notes on

      (a) Offences and, penalties under medical termination of pregnancies act.

(b) Medical Termination of pregnancies.

(c) Salient features of Medical termination of pregnancy Act.

5. Whether the termination of pregnancy under the following circumstances is legal or an offence under the act ? Discuss.

   (a) Termination of the pregnancy of a woman of 18 year of age without the consent of her guardian.

   (b) Termination of pregnancy of a woman 18½ years of age without the consent of her parents.

   (c) Termination of pregnancy at the residence of a registered medical practitioner.

Appendix

SCHEDULE A

FORM 1

Memorandum to the Central Drugs Laboratory)

Serial Number...................
To the Director, Central Drugs Laboratory........................
From ....

I send herewith, under the provisions of Section 25 (4) of the Drugs and Cosmetics Act, 1940, sample (s) of a drug purporting to be .... for test or analysis and request that a report of the result of the test or analysis may be supplied to this Court.

2. The distinguishing number on the packet is ....
3. Particulars of offence alleged ....
4. Matter on which opinion is required ....
5. A fee of Rs. .... has been deposited in Court.

Date ....

....
Magistrate

FORM 2

Certificate of test or analysis by the Central Drugs Laboratory

Certified that the samples, bearing number .... purporting to be a sample of .... received on .... with memorandum No................dated .... from ....has been tested/analysed and that the result of such test/analysis is as stated below :

2. The condition of the seals on the packet on receipt was as follow :

....

is of standard

3. In the opinion of the undersigned the sample....................

is not of standard

quality as defined in the Drugs and Cosmetics Act, 1940, and Rules quality as defined in the Drugs and Cosmetics Act, 1940, and Rules thereunder .... for the reasons given below :—

thereunder

Director,

Date.............Central Drugs Laboratory, or other authorised officer.

Details of results of test or analysis with protocols tests applied.

Director

Central Drugs Laboratory or other authorised officer.

FORM 8

Application for licence to import biological and other special products specified in Schedules C and C (1) (excluding those specified in Schedule X) to the Drugs and Cosmetic Rules, 1945.

I/We .... hereby apply for a licence to import the drugs specified below manufactured by ....of ....

Name of drugs and classes of drugs

I/We .... enclose herewith an undertaking signed by or on behalf of the manufacturers as required by the Drugs and Cosmetics Rules, 1945.

A fee of rupees fifty has been credited to Government under the head of Account (XXIII)—Medical—Miscellaneous—fees under the Drugs and Cosmetics Rules, 1945—Central *vide* treasury receipt attached.

Date................

Manufacturer's Agent

FORM 8A

Application for licence to import drugs specified in Schedule X to the Drugs and Cosmetics Rules, 1945.

I/We .... hereby apply for a licence to import drugs specified below manufactured by .... of ....

Name of the drugs and classes of drugs :

I/We .... enclose herewith an undertaking signed by or on behalf of the manufacturers as required by the Drugs and Cosmetics Rules, 1945.

A fee of rupees fifty has been credited to Government under the Head of Account '080-Medical-Miscellaneous-fee under the Drugs and Cosmetics Rules, 1945-Central' vide treasury receipt attached.

Date ....   Manufacturer's Agent.

FORM 9

Form of undertaking to accompany an application for an import licence

Whereas .... of .... intends to apply for a licence under the Drugs and Cosmetics Rules, 1945, for the import into India, of the drugs specified below manufactured by us, we.........................of ....hereby give this undertaking that for the duration of the said licence:—

(1) the said applicant shall be our agent for import of drugs into India;

(2) we shall comply with the conditions imposed on licence by (Rules 74 and 78) of the Drugs and Cosmetics Rules, 1945;

(3) we declare that we are carrying on the manufacture of the drugs mentioned in this undertaking at the premises specified below, and we shall from time to time report any change of premises on which manufactured will be carried on

and in the cases where manufacture is carried on in more than one factory any change in the distribution of functions between the factories :

(4) we shall comply with the provisions of Part IX of the Drugs an Cosmetics Rules, 1945;

(5) every drug manufactured by us for import under licence into India shall as regards strength, quality and purity conform with the provision of Chapter III of the Drugs and Cosmetics Act, 1940, and of the Drugs and Cosmetics Rules, 1945;

(6) we shall comply with such further requirements, if any, as may be specified by Rules, by the Central Government under the Act and of which the licensing authority has given to the licensee not less than four months notice.

Name of drugs and classes of drugs

Particulars of premises where manufacture is carried on.

Date......................

Signed by or on
behalf of the manufacturer.

FORM 10

Licence to import biological and other special products specified in Schedules C and C(I) (excluding those specified in Schedule X) to the Drugs and Cosmetics Rules, 1945

Number of licence ....of ....is/are hereby licensed to import into India during the period for which this licence is in force the drugs specified below manufactured by ....of .... and any other drugs manufactured by .... as may from time to time be endorsed on this licence.

(2) This is subject to the conditions prescribed in the Drugs and Cosmetics Rules, 1945, and shall be in force from

.... to ....unless it is sooner suspended or cancelled under the said Rules.

(3) The licensee shall inform the Licensing Authority in writing in the event to any change in the constitution of the firm operating under the licence. Where any change in the constitution of the firm takes place, the current licence shall be deemed to be valid for a maximum period of three months from the date on which the change takes place unless in the meantime a fresh licence has been taken from the Licensing Authority in the name of the firm with the changed constitution.)

Name of drugs and classes of drugs to which the licence applies

Date .... Licensing Authority

FORM 10-A

Licence to import drugs specified in Schedule X to the Drugs and Cosmetics Rules, 1945.

Number of Licence

1. .... is hereby licensed to import into India the period for which this licence is in force the drugs specified below manufactured by .... of .... and any other drugs manufactured by .... as may from time to time be endorsed on this licence.

2. This is subject to the conditions prescribed in the Drugs and Cosmetics Rules, 1945, and shall be in force from .... to .... unless it is sooner suspended or cancelled under the said rules.

Name of the drugs :

3. The licensee shall inform the licensing authority in writing in the event of any change in the constitution of the firm operating under the licence. Where any change in the constitution of the firm operating under the licence. Where any change in the constitution of the firms takes place, the current licence shall be deemed to be valid for a maximum period of three months from the date on which the change takes place unless in the meantime a fresh-licence has been taken from the licensing authority in the name of the firm with the changed constitution.

Date : Licensing Authority

FORM 11

Licence to import drugs for the purposes of examination, test or analysis

.... of .... is hereby licensed to import from .... the drugs specified below for the purposes of examination test or analysis at .... or in such other place as the licensing authority may from time to time authorize.

2. This licence is subject to the conditions prescribed in the Rules under the Drugs and Cosmetics Act, 1940.

3. This licence shall unless previously suspended or revoked be in force for a period of one year from the date specified below.

Name of Drugs **Quantities which may be imported**

Date .... Licensing Authority

FORM 12

Application for licence to import drugs for the purposes of examination test or analysis

I. .... resident of .... by occupation .... hereby apply for a licence to import the drugs specified below for the purpose of examination, test or analysis at .... applicable to the licence.

A fee of rupees fifteen has been credited to Government under the head of Account '080' Medical Miscellaneous fee under the Drugs and Cosmetics Rules, 1945—Central vide treasury receipt attached.

Name of drugs and classes of drugs **Quantities**

Date .... Signature....................

FORM 12-A

Application for the issue of a permit to import small quantities of drugs for personal use

I .... resident of .... by occupation .... hereby apply for a permit to import the drugs specified below for the personal use from ....

I attach a prescription from a registered medical practitioner in regard to the need for the said drugs.

Name of drugs **Quantities**

Date .... Signature ....

FORM 12-B

Permit for the import of small quantities of drugs for personal use

.... of .... is hereby permitted to import from .... the drugs specified below for the personal use.

2. This permit is subject to the conditions prescribed in the Rules under the Drugs and Cosmetics Act, 1940.

3. This permit shall, unless previously suspended or revoked be in force for a period of six months from the date specified below.

Name of drugs **Quantities which may be imported**

Date .... Licensing Authority

FORM 13

Certificate of test or analysis by Government Analyst under Section 25(1) of the Drugs and Cosmetics Act, 1940

1. Name of Inspector from whom received ....
2. Serial No. and date of Inspector's memorandum ....

3. Number of sample ....
4. Date of receipt ....
5. Name of drugs purporting to be contained in the sample ....
6. Condition of seals on the package ....
7. Result of test or analysis with (protocols of test or analysis) applied ....

is of

In the opinion of the undersigned the sample referred to above............

is not of

standard quality as defined in the Drugs and Cosmetics Act, 1940 and Rules standard quality as defined in the Drugs and Cosmetics Act, 1940 and Rules thereunder

.... for the reasons given below :

Date .... Government Analyst ....

FORM 13-A

Certificate of test or analysis by Government Analyst under Section 33H of the Drugs and Cosmetics Act, 1940.

1. Name of Inspector from whom received ....
2. Serial No. and date of Inspector's memorandum ....
3. Number of sample ....
4. Date of receipt ....
5. Names of ingredients purporting to have been used in the preparation of the sample ....
6. Conditions of seals on the package ....
7. Result of test or analysis with ....

Date .... Government ....

FORM 14-A

Application from a purchaser for test or analysis of a drug under Section 26 of the Drugs and Cosmetics Act, 1940.

1. Full name and address of the applicant ....
2. Occupation ....

3. Name of drug purporting to be contained in the sample.......
4. Name and full address of the pharmacy or concern where the drug was purchased ....
5. Date on which purchased ....
6. Reasons why the drug is being submitted for test or analysis ....
7. A fee of rupees .... *vide* Schedule B to the Drugs and Cosmetics Rules, 1945 has been credited to Government under the head of account "XXVII'—Medical—Miscellaneous—Fees under the Drugs and Cosmetics Rules, 1945—Central/State"—*vide* treasury receipt attached.

I hereby declare that the drug being submitted for test was purchased by or for me. I further declare that the sample of the drug being sent for test or analysis is exactly as it was purchased and has not been tampered within any way to reduce its potency.

Date .... Signed ....

FORM 14-B

Certificate of test or analysis by Government Analyst under Section 26 of the Drugs and Cosmetics Act, 1940

1. Name of person from whom sample received.
2. Date of receipt.
3. Name of drug purporting to be contained in the sample.

Opinion of the Government Analyst—The sample referred to above is/is not of standard quality as defined in the Drugs and Cosmetics Act, 1940, and Rules thereunder.

Date .... Government Analyst ....

FORM 19

Application for grant or renewal of a licence (to sell, stock, exhibit or offer for sale or distribution) of drugs other than those specified in Schedule X

1. I/We .... hereby apply for licence to sell by (wholesale/retail drugs specified in Schedules C and C(1)

excluding those specified in Schedule X and/or drugs other than those specified in Schedule C, C (1) and X to the Drugs and Cosmetics Rules, 1945 and also to operate a pharmacy on the premises situated at ....

2. (The sale and dispensing of drugs will be made under the personal supervision of a qualified person, namely :

(Name) ....(Qualification)
(Name) .... (Qualification)

3. Categories of drugs to be sold.

4. Particulars for special storage accommodation.

5. A fee of rupees .... has been credited to the Government account under the head of account ....

Date .... Signature ....

FORM 19-A

Application for grant or renewal of a restricted licence to sell, stock, exihibit (or offer for) sale, or distribute drugs by retail by (tinerant vendors and other dealers who do not engage the services of a qualified person.)

1. I/We ....of .... hereby
(Drugs other than those specified
apply for a licence to sell by retail (i) ....
Drugs other than those specified
in Schedule C, C(1) and X) on the premises situated at ....
in Schedule C,C(I) and X) as vendor in the area ....
Drugs specified in (Schedule C(1) on the premises situated at
or (ii) ....
Drugs specified in Schedule C(1) as vendor in the area.

2. Sales shall be restricted to such drugs as can be sold without the supervision of a qualified person under the Drugs and Cosmetics Rules.

3. Names or classes of drugs proposed to be sold ....

4. Particulars of the storage accommodation for the storage of [Schedule C(1)] drugs on premises referred to above.

5. The drugs for the sale will be purchased from the following dealers and such other dealers as may be endorsed on the licence by the licensing authority for time to time.

Name of dealers .... Licence No. ....

6. A fee of rupees $\frac{\text{five}}{\text{twenty}}$ has been credited to Government under the head of account ....

Date .... Signature ....

FORM 19-AA

Application for grant or renewal of a licence (to sell, stock, exhibit or offer for sale by wholesale or to distribute) drugs from a motor vehicle.

1. I/We .... of ....hereby apply for licence to sell by wholesale or to distribute drugs specified in Schedule C and schedule C (1) and/or drugs other than those specified in Schedule C and Schedule C(1) from the vehicle bearing No. .... assigned under the Motor Vehicles Act, 1939.

2. Categories of drugs to be sold/distributed ....

3. A fee of rupees .... has been credited to Government under the head of account.

4. Particulars of the storage accommodation for the storage of drugs specified in Schedule C and C(1) on the vehicle referred to above.

Date .... Signature ....

FORM 19-C

Application for grant or renewal of a licence (to sell, stock, exhibit or offer for sale or distribution) of drugs specified in Schedule X

1. I/We .... of .... hereby apply for a licence to wholesale/retail drugs specified in Schedule X to the Drugs and Cosmetics Rules, 1945. We operate a pharmacy on the premises, situated at ....

2. The sale and dispensing of drugs will be made under the personal supervision of the qualified persons mentioned below :

(Name) .... (Qualification).
(Name) .... (Qualification).
3. Name of drugs to be sold.
4. Particulars of storage accommodation.
5. A fee of rupees .... has been credited to Government account under the head of account ....

Date .... Signature ....

FORM 20

Licence (to sell, stock, exhibit or offer for sale or distribute) drugs by retail other than those specified in [Schedules C,C (1) and X]

I ....is hereby licensed to sell, stock or exhibit for sale or distribute by retail drugs other than those specified in [Schedules C, C(1) and X] of the Drugs and Cosmetics Rules, 1945, (and to operate a pharmacy on the premises situated at .... subject to the conditions specified below and to the provisions of the Drugs and Cosmetics Act, 1940 and the Rules thereunder.

2. The licence shall be in force from .... to ....
3. Name (s) of qualified person (s) in charge ....
4. Categories of drugs ....
(Date ....Licence No. .... Licensing Authority)

FORM 20-A

Restricted licence (to sell, stock, exhibit or offer for sale or distribute) drugs by retail other than those specified in [Schedule C, C(1) and X] for itinerant vendors and other dealers who do not engage the services of a qualified person.

1. I .... is hereby licensed to sell, stock or exhibit for sale or distribute on premises situated at/as vendor in the area ....(the following drugs being drugs other than) those specified in [Schedule C, C (I) and X] of the Drugs and Cosmetics Rules, 1945 subject to the condition specified below and to provisions of the Drugs and Cosmetics Act, 1940 and Rules made thereunder.

2. The licence shall be in force from .... to ....

3. The licensee can deal only in such drugs as can be sold without the supervision of a 'qualified person' under the Drugs and Cosmetics 1945.

4. The licensee, if he be an itinerant vendor, shall buy drugs only from the following dealers and such other dealers as may be endorsed on the licence by Licensing Authority from time to time.

Name of the dealer .... Licence No. ....

Date .... Licensing Authority

FORM 20-B

Licence (to sell, stock, exhibit or offer for sale or distribute by wholesale, drugs other than those specified in [Schedules C,C (1) andX]

1. I .... is hereby licensed to sell, stock or exhibit for sale or distribute by wholesale drugs other than those specified in [Schedules C, C (1) and X] on the premises situated at .... subject to the conditions specified below and to the provisions of the Drugs and Cosmetics Act, 1940, and the Rules thereunder.

2. The licence shall be in force from .... to ....

3. Categories of drugs ....

Date .... Licence No. Licensing Authority

FORM 20-B

Licence (to sell, stock, or exhibit or offer for sale by wholesale or to distribute) drugs other than those specified in Schedule C and Schedule C (1) to the Drugs and Cosmetics Rules, 1945 from a motor vehicle.

1. .... is hereby licensed to sell by wholesale or to distribute drugs other than those specified in Schedule C and Schedule C (1) from the vehicle bearing registration No. .... assigned under Motor Vehicles Act, 1939, subject to the conditions specified below and to the provisions of the Drugs and Cosmetics Act, 1940 and the Rules made thereunder.

2. The licence shall be in force from .... to ....

3. Categories of drugs ....

Date ....

Licence No.

Licensing Authority